Enhancing Your Personality for God

by

Prince Yinka Oyekan

17 High Cross Street
St. Austell, Cornwall
England
PL25 4AN
Tel: (01726) 72282

Seedtime Publishing

Seedtime Publishing
17 High Cross Street
St. Austell
Cornwall PL25 4AN
England

Copyright © 1995 Yinka Oyekan

All rights reserved. No part of this publication may be reproduced, stored in a retrieval system, or transmitted in any form or by any means, electronic, mechanical, photocopying or otherwise, without the prior written consent of the publisher.

Short extracts may be quoted for review purposes.

All Scripture quotations are taken from the NIV, The Holy Bible, New International Verion unless otherwise stated.
Copyright © 1973, 1978 International Bible Society. Published by Hodder & Stoughton.

ISBN 0 9525396 0 8

Typeset by CRB Associates, Lenwade, Norwich, England
Printed by Clays Ltd, St. Ives plc

Acknowledgement

To Fiona, my wife.

Thanks for all the input and help.

Contents

PART A:
Understanding Your Personality
from the Scriptures   7

Chapter 1   The Need for Biblical Understanding   9

Chapter 2   The Mirror of the Personality   17

Chapter 3   Purposeful Personalities   39

PART B:
How to Enhance Your Personality   55

Chapter 4   Redirecting, Reseating and Anchoring Our Will and Emotions   57

Chapter 5   Developing a Faith-Filled Personality   69

Chapter 6   Developing a Joy and Praise-Filled Personality   87

Chapter 7   Acquired Characteristics   103

Chapter 8   Developing a Spirit of Excellence   125

Chapter 9   Personality and Appearance   145

            Appendix   153

PART A:

Understanding Your Personality from the Scriptures

Chapter 1

The Need for Biblical Understanding

Why should Christians be bothered about personality? The answer is clear. When a person's personality is transformed by God the change is always glorious. Repentant prostitutes become pillars of society. Homosexuals acknowledge and repent of their sin; they sometimes get married and prove to be good fathers and husbands. Change is not only reserved for the grossly immoral unbeliever who repents. Christians who are committed to the Word and Spirit of God can also have their personalities transformed from one degree of glory to another (2 Corinthians 3:18). But, most people have had their views on personality shaped by the world and it has led to a culture overwhelmingly concerned with self, a 'what is in it for me' approach to Christianity. Nevertheless personality is important, and as a consequence many believers will rightly try to understand what personality means. What has shaped your view, has it been the world or the word of God?

What is Personality

> *'When you study what is real you study reality. When you study what the Bible says about the person you study personality.'*

It is what the Bible says a person is that determines what personality means. Unlike psychology the Bible does not limit personality to the inner workings of a man's mind. The Bible looks upon man as a whole integral being. It speaks about aspects or traits belonging to that being which gives us insight into that specific person. When we study those words or adjectives used to describe the person I believe that we are studying personality. For example most people think of personality as being a person's character. They then include the soulish expression of that person and consider that to be the sum of his personality. Both of these things are just an aspect or part of the whole picture. I was amazed to find out that a person's looks, job and even status are considered in the scriptures to be as much a part of that individual's personal expression of himself as the expression of the soul is. There are many words in both Greek and Hebrew that could be translated *'person'*. The Greek word for soul, for instance, can be translated life, mind or person. The Hebrew word for countenance can be translated visage, face or person. The Bible uses different words and adjectives to describe a person, depending on what aspect of the person it wishes to bring out of the whole picture. So to study what the Bible says about *'person'*, and to consider the adjectives used to describe *'person'* is to study personality from a biblical perspective. The wonderful thing is that there is not an aspect of the person that cannot be transformed and enhanced, whether it is a person's looks, job or expression of his soul. But this is only possible when the person is willing to yield his or her life to God and obey His word. Psychology may well have **some truth** to share about the inner workings of the mind, but only the word of God will give *'the truth'* and the kind of insight and understanding that we need in order to become attractive personalities for God. If we simply want wonderful personalities so that we, rather than God, stand out then God's Spirit cannot easily transform the aspects that need enhancing for God. It is possible to impress because we have used self-help techniques that cause us to stand out from the crowd. Many do such things because they are vain and want to look good, but this does not impress God and it is not what God desires for us.

The amazing transformation of an individual's personality when they come into a knowledge of Jesus Christ as Lord and Saviour is startling. After that initial and total surrender they are markedly changed. Do you remember the first time you led someone to Christ and saw an amazing alteration in their nature? They suddenly become attractive personalities to both Christians and unbelievers alike. This amazing butterfly-like metamorphosis seemed to take place all within a very short space of time. When questioned closely, I have found that a lot of mature Christians often feel that they have lost a certain amount of this attractiveness and would love to regain it, while others think that their demeanour has not undergone the kind of transformation that it should have and consequently surmise that their personality hinders them.

I was amazed at the example of James (please note that all names given in a single form in this book have been changed and circumstances slightly altered to protect identities). James is an extreme case but he does illustrate the problems some people face. He so disliked his personality that at times his frustration caused him to lose control of his temper provoking him to break some of his furniture in sheer frustration. A couple of times he confessed to me that he harboured the thought of suicide. He believed that he had an unattractive personality and longed to have what he considered to be an attractive one. This is a basic desire that is found in most of us. Few people would want a repulsive personality.

Like James, as we look around us we realise that *'Attractiveness is the means by which relationships are initiated'*. This is a principle written into the whole of creation. A bee will spot a flower and be attracted to it in the hope of acquiring nectar. The Earth exerts a different kind of attractiveness on the Moon called gravity. Whether this attraction is an attraction to a set of ideas, an object or attraction to a member of the opposite sex, attractiveness brings things into relationship. When Adam saw Eve he was overcome with affection. God realised he was lonely and wanted to reveal this to Adam (Genesis 2:18), and so God asked Adam to name all the animals, which he did, but by the time he had accomplished this task he would have realised that every animal in the whole of creation either had a mate or some other means by which it could reproduce, except himself.

> *'So the man gave names to all the livestock, the birds of the air and all the beasts of the field. But for Adam no suitable helper was found.'* (Genesis 2:20)

It is obvious that by the end of the naming task he had begun his search for a suitable helper. He was certainly not getting hitched to a hippopotamus or a donkey, the former being thick skinned the latter being stubborn. They would not have appealed to him as being attractive. God, having helped him discover his loneliness, then put him into a deep sleep, removed part of his side and formed Eve. The minute Adam saw Eve he burst into what are the very first ever lines of poetry.

> *'The man said, "This is now bone of my bones and flesh of my flesh; she shall be called 'woman', for she was taken out of man."'* (Genesis 2:23)

Where he was not tempted to set up home with a giraffe or aroused to seek companionship with a donkey or awakened to new feelings of affection by the sight of an elephant he was romantically stirred and moved to high praise by the sight of Eve. And ever since men have been writing love letters to possible spouses which are more often an embarrassment to the intellect than a work of art, but nevertheless each romantic scribble provides a source of joy to the emotions of the recipient and the sender. He was attracted to Eve and as a result a relationship was initiated. Thus man continues to long for an attractive personality because instinctively we know it is the means by which relationships are initiated. Even Jesus prayed for the church that the unity within the church would be a source of amazement to the

The Need for Biblical Understanding

world and thus initiate an attraction. He even placed his glory upon the church in order that this state of unity might come about (John 17:20–23).

> *'My prayer is not for them alone. I pray also for those who will believe in me through their message,* [21] *that all of them may be one, Father, just as you are in me and I am in you. May they also be in us so that the world may believe that you have sent me.* [22] *I have given them the glory that you gave me, that they may be one as we are one.'* (John 17:20–22)

Jesus' prayer was that His church would be attractive to the lost, and so there is absolutely nothing wrong with the desire for an attractive personality. Everyone has personality. The important questions are (a) what does the Bible say personality is and (b) can it be transformed into an attractive and enhanced personality, not for our own gain but for God and His glory?

It is possible to have this attractive personality that reflects the glory of God, but we must be prepared to hear from God's word what we need to hear and not just what we want to hear. If God's word is not implanted in our lives our personalities cannot mature. Jesus made it clear that growth and maturity requires freedom for the word of God to take root.

> *'The seed that fell among thorns stands for those who hear, but as they go on their way they are choked by life's worries, riches and pleasures, and they do not* ***mature.****'* (Luke 8:14)

To have a developed personality means that we will have to be wholeheartedly committed to what the word of God says about the changes that need to take place in our personalities. Many of the chapters of this book will challenge a lot of our previously held views. They will require a great deal of resolve to put into practice, but if we are willing to embrace what the Lord has to say, then we will find that He will help us achieve maturity in our personality. If we are not influenced in our thinking by the word of God then we will be influenced adversely by what the world is now teaching about personality. If we are not careful it will not be long before we are also found to be saying, *'I can not help myself because God made me this way'*.

The Impact of a Worldly Perspective

The common factor that ties the world's perspective on personality together is that they are usually Human-centric rather than Theo-centric. They encourage us to put ourselves at the centre of our thinking rather than to put God at the centre of our thought life. They seek to convince us that if we put ourselves at the centre of our thinking we will achieve maturity. This is the very sin that the Devil used to entice Adam and Eve in the garden of Eden. God had told Adam and Eve that they must not eat of the tree in the garden. This was the **word of God** to them. But the Devil wanted to destroy their confidence in God's word. He encouraged them to put their desires before God's word. His promise to them was that if they ate of the fruit they would be like God.

> *'The woman said to the serpent, "We may eat fruit from the trees in the garden,* [3] *but God did say, 'You must not eat fruit from the tree that is in the middle of the garden, and you must not touch it, or you will die.'"* [4] *"You will not surely die," the serpent said to the woman.* [5] *"For God knows that when you eat of it your eyes will be opened, and you will be like God, knowing good and evil."'* (Genesis 3:2–5)

The Devil was able to convince Adam and Eve that they would achieve *'greater self realization'* if they ate the fruit, as he put it *'your eyes will be opened'*. The consequence of accepting this lie and rejecting the word of God was that the whole of their being was tainted with sin. Rather than growing in their personality they became stunted in their growth. Another word was implanted into their life not God's. The Devil has not stopped using this concept. What is the cry of this age? Is it not still the same *'put yourself first'* mentality? The Devil has primarily promoted the idea through false religions, therefore at the centre of many mystical cults and religions one finds the idea of *'self realization'* to be at the core of its philosophy. For instance, self realization as taught by the New Age Movement is seen by millions as the only means by which the individual will ultimately achieve spirituality. In fact one of the greatest evils according to New Age Teaching is an individual not realising he is a god. Is this not what the political, social and secular society also impresses upon the individual?

The lack of clear scriptural teaching about what personality is and should be used for coupled with acceptance of the world's views on personality has resulted in some churches being filled with individuals more concerned about what they can get out of God, church or others rather than what they can give to God. Since the Garden of Eden mankind has continued to be obsessed about *'self'*, and wants to understand what he can or cannot achieve. Psychologists have tried to understand the very deep inner identity and workings of an individual's mind and personality. The problem is, it lacks a scriptural content or emphasis. Worse still it lacks a scriptural basis. Psychologists, by definition, are limited to the workings of the mind, whilst a person is made up of body, soul and spirit. To fully appreciate personality we need a full scriptural understanding of who God made us and why He made us. The question is not *'how can we improve ourselves?'*, because this motivation can be selfish, but *'how can we serve and fulfil God's will and purpose for our lives?'*. If we adopt this approach our personalities can be enhanced for God and the contents of this book will help you.

Chapter 2

The Mirror of the Personality

In this chapter please take great care to consider every italicised word as they denote subtle but important connotations.

What View Do We Have of Ourselves?

How we see ourselves is important. A wrong view of ourselves can hinder the development of our personality towards maturity. If we are to enhance our personality for God then we must face who and what we really are. If we have a wrong perspective about ourselves we could say that we are deceived. Deceived people behave in strange ways. We read of people who under the influence of drugs have leaped out of windows thinking they could fly. They were deceived by the drug. Similarly if we are deceived about the scope of our personalities we will behave in inappropriate or limited ways. Satan is one culprit who tries to get us to picture ourselves through crooked glasses. The way other people see us can also *'influence'* the development of our personalities. The important perspective that we need to pay attention to is the one God has of us, what He wants us to be like and where we are on that journey to maturity. Taking responsibility for our current growth or lack of it in our personality is the starting point to enhancing it for God.

The Source of Personality

(a) Do genes, culture and background 'determine' personality?

What is the source of our personality? I have heard people excuse their children's bad temper by saying *'he gets it from his father'*. By this some parents have meant that the child was simply copying his father but I have also heard mothers say this and mean by it that the problem was genetic. Periodically, as adults, we attempt to shrug off some of our *'faults'* because we believe they have been genetically passed down to us by our parents. But does this stand up to Scripture? I believe that genetically we can pick up a *'mannerism'* from our parents or acquire one because we have chosen to copy them, but I do not believe that we can delegate responsibility for our *'faults'* to genetics. A *'mannerism'* is totally different to a *'fault'* as an individual's faults are down to his or her personal choice. But what does Scripture say? Is the source of our personality the result of some genetic union spouting from our parents? If this were the case then it would be true to say that people could not help some of their sins because they were genetic. Experience in counselling and more importantly *'the word of God'* shows us that genes cannot of their own accord *'determine'* the personality of an individual (Ezekiel 18). If we conclude that genes cannot *'determine'* a person's personality we are saying that though the person's genes may *'influence'* mannerisms they cannot take away an individual's free choice and thus *'determine'* his personality. This is seen in the story of Jacob and Esau.

Jacob and Esau were twins, and perhaps one would have expected very similar personality traits between the two brothers (even though they were not identical twins). If genes absolutely *'determined'* behaviour regardless of choice then Jacob and Esau would have been very similar in the expression of their personality. In Scripture we find that the opposite is true. They were as different as chalk is to cheese. Jacob was a homely man who was extremely deceptive and calculating. His twin brother Esau was an adventurer who

The Mirror of the Personality

was rash, rough and rugged. From their example we can see that though genes *'may affect'* us physically by highlighting family characteristics or resemblance, genes do not determine personality. If genes *'determined'* personality they should have been much more alike. The kind of sins that we put down to genes cannot be palmed off as the fault of our parents. We are Adam's offspring but we don't have to follow in our father's footsteps. The second thing of interest that Jacob and Esau's circumstances show us is that their environment did not play a major part in *'determining'* their personalities. The two boys were brought up within the same culture, home, nation, time, they even shared the same birthday, and yet they had completely different dispositions.

This is important to note because some psychologists try to lead us to believe that an individual's personality is *'determined'* by his home, culture, class and background. Fortunately the word of God shows us again and again that though personality is *'shaped'* by culture or background our personality is not ultimately *'subject'* to our circumstances but is rather subject to our *'choices'*. I cannot stress the importance of distinguishing between the ability of a parent to *'influence'* a child and their inability to *'determine'* a child's personality.

I heard an interesting story which illustrates this. Two brothers had turned out very differently, one was an alcoholic the other a high achieving teetotaller. Both had suffered the tyranny of their alcoholic father. When asked the question 'why do you think you have turned out the way you have?' they both gave this answer 'with a father like I had what would you expect?'. Both had been *'influenced'* by their father but it would not be true to say that their father had *'determined'* their personality. The brothers' personalities had been *'determined'* by their own individual choices. The one who became an alcoholic had chosen to follow his father's bad example having been adversely *'influenced'* by his father who he blamed for his condition. The other brother had also been *'influenced'*, but rather than allow his negative upbringing to *'determine'* a pattern for his life he chose to avoid the mistakes of his father and made a positive life for himself. Some of the kings of Israel are spoken of in a similar manner. In the book of Kings we read that some of the kings followed in their father's wicked footsteps and others did not (1 Kings 15:26, 1 Kings 22:52, 2 Kings 3:2, 2 Kings 21:20, 2 Kings 24:9). The choice is always the individual's and not down to genetic makeup.

Some psychologists have tried to blame parents for the myriad of problems that children frequently have, but even though this is often true in part, the fact is that parental incompetence cannot be the final or ultimate reason why an individual has a particular personality. Adam and Eve were the first parents ever. It would be convenient to blame them for Cain murdering his brother Abel, but God does not. God firmly puts the blame at Cain's feet. Yes, parents can be incompetent but the child still makes his own choices and decisions and must account for them. A bad upbringing can leave a person with many scars and many hurts, but for every individual who is overcome by ill-treatment there are individuals who, like Joseph, refuse to allow the bad upbringing to *'determine'* what they are presently like. Joseph was mentally abused (Genesis 37:23, 28), physically abused (Genesis 39:20), and he was sexually harassed (Genesis 39:7–10). He was lied about, rejected and imprisoned. Joseph was forced into slavery and denied his freedom yet in all his hardship and turbulent upbringing he walked with God and did not harbour bitterness or unforgiveness in his heart. How many people have you met who have had to undergo what Joseph went through? This kind of straight soul-searching approach to this subject can appear cold but we cannot really deny that it is true. When the truth is shared in the love of Christ true liberty can flow. We therefore need to be careful about who or what we attribute sin to. Saying that an individual's personality is **'genetically determined'** or to say a person cannot help their personality because God made them that way, or even to say it is the result of background, parents, culture etc., is the same thing as saying that the individual who sins has got no choice in the matter, and he has been genetically engineered without any possibility of choosing to be different. Some people take Psalm 139:13–16 as their proof text to indicate that we are created robots without choice as to what personality we have.

> *'For you created my inmost being; you knit me together in my mother's womb.* [14] *I praise you because I am fearfully and wonderfully made; your works are wonderful, I know that full well.* [15] *My frame was not hidden from you when I was made in the secret place. When I was woven together in the depths of the earth,* [16] *your eyes saw my unformed body. All the days ordained for me were written in your book before one of them came to be.'*
>
> (Psalm 139:13–16)

But the fact is these verses simply show us that God created us and gave us life and made us unique individuals. It does not mean that He has fixed and imprinted our personalities upon us, it just means that He has ordained the number of days we will live and knows everything about us. He makes us wonderful not terrible. **'No-one ever makes anything to function badly, we all want our creations to work efficiently'**. God did not make us bad. It would be unfair of God to send anyone to hell if our sinful actions were purely the result of how He has made us. Obviously God does not put sin down to some genetic disorder, and He has said He will send people who do not repent of sin to hell. **'Everything can influence our personality but only one thing can determine our personality'**, and this is what we will now go on to look at.

(b) The determiner of Personality

So what determines personality if it not **'determined'** by genetics? The **'word of God'** shows us that expressed personality is that which is shaped by our choices in life. It is not fixed at birth but is learned. Just like we learn to walk by process of trial and error until it becomes habitual normal behaviour, we learn to behave in particular ways until it becomes habitual and normal. It is this normal habitual behaviour that people recognise as missing when it is thought that a person is behaving *'out of character'*. What we mean when we make such comments is that the individual is not behaving in a manner we would normally expect. We recognise and categorise people by their normal behaviour patterns. And so we can recognise extroverts and introverts, and guess roughly how they might behave in a given situation. ***'Personality is the pattern of behaviour we have learned to express by choice'***. I remember when I was a little boy of seven years my grandmother used to say of me ***'Yinka never lies'***. This caused me to feel so good about myself that I never ever remember telling her anything but the truth. Of course I did lie to my friends at times like most other young boys, but I always remembered to take care not to lie to my grandmother. She *'influenced'* my behaviour but I determined how I would behave. Once I had established the pattern it did not take much effort to continue telling her the truth. We all learn to mould our mind into a pattern which becomes a habitual way of thinking and behaving and so the scripture says we should be transformed by the renewing of our mind.

> *'Therefore, I urge you, brothers, in view of God's mercy, to offer your bodies as living sacrifices, holy and pleasing to God – this is your spiritual act of worship. ^{2} Do not conform any longer to the pattern of this world, but be transformed by the renewing of your mind. Then you will be able to test and approve what God's will is – his good, pleasing and perfect will.'* (Romans 12:1–2)

It is possible to change and enhance our expressed personality because all that is required is a change in our will. The pattern of behaviour or the way we express our personality at this present time has been influenced by many things but ultimately it has been determined by our will. Scripturally speaking our attitudes, behaviour and choices in life are all down to our will, Scripture placing the onus of responsibility for actions firmly on the individual. It is only after taking responsibility for our actions that we can hope to deal with things like circumstances, culture or background which *'influence'* our will and thus our personality but cannot be blamed for *'determining'* our will and thus our personality. In a man's struggle to make decisions the will is influenced in its options because *'the will is only as powerful as that which we allow to exert the most force on it'*. We make selections based on the things that exercise the greatest influence on our will and so our convictions, fears, culture, circumstances or even other people will influence our behaviour, **BUT** other people, circumstances and culture are not *'responsible'* for, nor can they 'determine' our choices or personality.

(c) Discovering the seat of the will

In order to make His hearers take note Jesus used different Greek words for life to show what was governing the will or in other words where the will was seated. Jesus, in doing this, reveals that the will can be seated in different places and is consequently influenced by where it finds its seat. One word He used to describe what could govern our will was the Greek word *'bios'*. It is from *'bios'* that we get the word **'biology'** or *'biological'*. The sense of the word *'bios'* means *'the present state of basic fleshly requirements and the resources or desires needed to maintain this kind of lifestyle'*. The word is translated *'life'* or *'living'*. Let us call this type of life *'bios life'* for shortness. This is the word that Jesus used in the story of the woman with the issue of blood.

> *'And a woman was there who had been subject to bleeding for twelve years.* [26] *She had suffered a great deal under the care of many doctors and had spent all she had* (bios), *yet instead of getting better she grew worse.'*
> (Mark 5:24–26)

He highlighted the fact that she lived a *'bios life'*, and had spent all her *'living'* (*bios*), or the resources by which she maintained herself, primarily on securing the help of doctors. The influence our physical requirements put on our lives can be incredible and Jesus showed that her principal consideration was practical and physical. But He warned that there was a negative side to this kind of lifestyle. If the seat of our will was to be found in our physical realm then it could choke the process of maturing within our life.

> *'The seed that fell among thorns stands for those who hear, but as they go on their way they are choked by life's* (bios) *worries, riches and pleasures, and they do not mature.* [15] *But the seed on good soil stands for those with a noble and good heart, who hear the word, retain it, and by persevering produce a crop.'* (Luke 8:14–15)

Jesus made it clear **'bios dominated life'** or the lifestyle that is primarily concerned with the present state of basic fleshly requirements can choke the reception and growth of the word in our life. This is because the personality dominated by the physical realm is basic, can be lustful and greedy for more and thus finds it hard to retain God's word. Peter also used the word *'bios'* when speaking about those who lived a life which showed that the seat of the will was being controlled by fleshly, basic desires.

> *'For you have spent enough time in the past doing what pagans choose to do – living* (bios) *in debauchery, lust, drunkenness, orgies, carousing and detestable idolatry.'*
> (1 Peter 4:3)

He is saying that we should not choose to live a life which allows lusts of the flesh to dominate our wills. It is true that the body has many appetites and some of them are needs without which life would be impossible. The danger is these desires can become lusts and dominate our will and influence our choices and thus our personality. Sex, for instance, is a physical need in people, the pinnacle of physical contact between two married human beings, but if we live fleshly lives Peter warns that we will end up in idolatry worshipping the physical needs by allowing them to dictate to our wills. We have an appetite which tells us that we need to eat but if we allow our appetite to control us then our will becomes dominated by the flesh and we will overindulge. The body has many tastes and needs, therefore *'bios life'* must be under control. When it is not, it becomes a source of boasting for the sinful man.

> *'For everything in the world – the cravings of sinful man, the lust of his eyes and the boasting of **what he has and does** (bios) –comes not from the Father but from the world.'* (1 John 2:16)

Another way of translating the emphasised portion of this verse would be to say *'the boasting of his life'*. The sinful man boasts about his material possessions and the means he possesses to maintain his existence, but believers are to have a different approach to *'bios life'*; they are to live quietly and at peace with their neighbours.

> *'I urge, then, first of all, that requests, prayers, intercession and thanksgiving be made for everyone –* [2] *for kings and all those in authority, that we may live peaceful and quiet lives* (bios) *in all godliness and holiness.* [3] *This is good, and pleases God our Saviour,* [4] *who wants all men to be saved and to come to a knowledge of the truth.'* (1 Timothy 2:1–4)

The second word that Jesus uses to indicate what could govern the individual's will and consequently affects his lifestyle and shapes his personality is the Greek word *'psyche'*. This word is used to indicate the personality that is concerned with the emotional, sensual or mental aspects of life. It is translated *'heart, soul, life or mind'*. It is perhaps the biggest influence on our wills because right at the beginning of creation man was created a *'living soul'* (Genesis 2:7), and so Adam is compared to Jesus.

> *'So it is written: "The first man Adam became a living being"* (psyche or soul); *the last Adam, a life-giving spirit.'*   (1 Corinthians 15:45)

The soul of man is the natural overriding disposition. If the seat of the will is based in the soulish realm the kind of personality that is expressed is either emotional or intellectual. The difficulty with this is that when the adamic soulish nature dominates, it comes into conflict with the spirit and will ultimately seek to counterfeit the work of the spirit. It is from the word *'psyche'* that we get the word *'psychology'*, which is the science that studies the mind, and the reasons why people think and act in particular ways. The word *'psychic'* is another word which comes from *'psyche'*. As we know psychics are busy trying to contact the spiritual world. The example of psychics tells us that without due care the *'psyche'* or soul will attempt to dominate the spiritual and imitate it. Psychics do not understand the dangers involved in trying to dominate the spiritual by means of the soulish. It then becomes obvious why many who play with ouija boards end up with terrible emotional problems. Because the soul and the mind are interlinked, any mental sins will leave the individual struggling and suffering emotionally. This is also why people get under great emotional and mental stress when they have been involved in transcendental meditation, yoga or other mind altering states. They get into emotional turmoil because the mind is so much one with the soul that the same word can be used to indicate those two aspects of man. The man who lives a purely soulish life can be deceived into thinking that he is being spiritual when he is purely following his own natural instincts.

> *'But, dear friends, remember what the apostles of our Lord Jesus Christ foretold.* [18] *They said to you, "In the last times there will be scoffers who will follow their own ungodly desires."* [19] *These are the men who divide you, who follow mere natural* (psychikos, or soulish) *instincts and do not have the Spirit.* [20] *But you, dear friends, build*

> *yourselves up in your most holy faith and pray in the Holy Spirit.'* (Jude 17–20)

Believers are to avoid this trap. We are to build ourselves up in the Holy Spirit not allowing our wills to be influenced by ungodly desires. Soulish dominated personalities are in danger of not receiving the things that come from the Lord nor can they understand them because man needs the Holy Spirit to understand the spiritually discernable.

> *'Which things also we speak, not in the words which man's wisdom teacheth, but which the Holy Ghost teacheth; comparing spiritual things with spiritual.* [14] *But the natural* (**psychikos**, or **soulish**) *man receiveth not the things of the Spirit of God: for they are foolishness unto him: neither can he know them, because they are spiritually discerned.'* (1 Corinthians 2:13–14 KJV)

James also warns against being soulish whilst thinking you are being spiritual.

> *'But if you harbour bitter envy and selfish ambition in your hearts, do not boast about it or deny the truth.* [15] *Such "wisdom" does not come down from heaven but is earthly, unspiritual* (psychikos, or soulish), *of the devil.* [16] *For where you have envy and selfish ambition, there you find disorder and every evil practice.'* (James 3:14–16)

He makes it clear that the source of a soulish dominated lifestyle, which includes attitudes such as selfish ambition, bitterness or envy is not spiritual or from heaven. The warning is not to be dominated by the soul whilst thinking it is the spirit nor to be taken in by people who appear to be spiritual but are actually soulish. Such people will often have a hidden agenda because soulish dominated people are mainly concerned with *'self'* and so primarily talk about *'I'*. It is not the things, people or events that surround *'the self'* that are important but *'I and only I'*. It is this soulish self-importance that eventually leads to such individuals competing against and counterfeiting the Holy Spirit by being *'psychikos'* or soulish.

The soulish life alienated from God is really no life at all. It covets and lusts for what it should not. This was the case with King David's son Amnon. He violated his sister Tamar, after falling in love with her (2 Samuel 13:14). He was being purely selfish as is the case when the will is dominated by the soul. King David's son paid no regard to the consequences of his actions for the girl. He was only concerned with gratifying his desire. Similarly when Samson eventually gave in to Delilah and revealed the source of his strength the scripture says *'She probed him day after day until his **soul** was vexed unto death'* (Judges 16:16 KJV). Whereas physically he could not be overcome, Delilah was able to overcome him emotionally.

The power of the soul lies in its ability to make us feel good or bad about an event or person. Thus even people who appear to be doing good works can be doing it not because they care for the other person who is on the receiving end, nor as a consequence or recognising that it is the right thing to do, but simply because they get something emotional out of doing their good works. I believe Peter once reacted in this manner. When Jesus told Peter that He was going to be put to death at the hands of the priests, Peter's response was emotional. He rebuked Jesus for suggesting such a thing.

> *'From that time on Jesus began to explain to his disciples that he must go to Jerusalem and suffer many things at the hands of the elders, chief priests and teachers of the law, and that he must be killed and on the third day be raised to life.* [22] *Peter took him aside and began to rebuke him. "Never, Lord!" he said. "This shall never happen to you!"* [23] *Jesus turned and said to Peter, "Get behind me, Satan! You are a stumbling block to me; you*

The Mirror of the Personality

> *do not have in mind the things of God, but the things of men."* ²⁴ *Then Jesus said to his disciples, "If anyone would come after me, he must deny himself and take up his cross and follow me.* ²⁵ *For whoever wants to save his life will lose it, but whoever loses his life for me will find it.* ²⁶ *What good will it be for a man if he gains the whole world, yet forfeits his soul? Or what can a man give in exchange for his soul?* ²⁷ *For the Son of Man is going to come in his Father's glory with his angels, and then he will reward each person according to what he has done.* ²⁸ *I tell you the truth, some who are standing here will not taste death before they see the Son of Man coming in his kingdom."'*
> (Matthew 16:21–28)

Jesus in turn corrected him in front of the disciples and highlighted the root of Peter's problem. Yes, it is true that Satan had inspired Peter's outburst but the root of the problem lay in Peter's soulish realm. Thus the challenge **'whoever wants to save his life** (psyche, soul)**'** will lose it. The subtlety of this challenge could be so easily lost in the translation. A paraphrase of Matthew 16:24–26 could read

> *'For whoever wants to save his soulish, emotional expression of life, will lose it, but whoever loses the soulish, emotional expression of his life for me, will find it.* ²⁶ *What good will it be for a man if he gains the whole world, yet forfeits his soul? Or what can a man give in exchange for his soul?'*
> (Matthew 16:24–26)

Jesus was rebuking Peter for yielding temporarily to the Devil to whom he was in danger of forfeiting his soul. There are echoes on verse 26 of Jesus' temptation at the hands of the Devil where He was offered the kingdoms of the earth. Jesus quite clearly demanded that Peter should rather lose his soul for Him rather than for what he might think he would gain if Jesus was not killed. Here is the power of the soul exposed. Peter was rebuking Jesus because of how he felt. The problem is that where the soul is dominant over a man's spirit the personality is motivated in a self-centred direction rather than a Godward direction. Jesus was very much aware of how great an influence the soul was when the will was seated in the soulish realm, and so He took time to warn His followers not to succumb to emotional considerations. We are not even to be afraid of people who could make life difficult for us because at the end of the day even if they kill us they cannot destroy our soul.

> *'What I tell you in the dark, speak in the daylight; what is whispered in your ear, proclaim from the roofs.* [28] *Do not be afraid of those who kill the body but cannot kill the soul. Rather, be afraid of the One who can destroy both soul and body in hell.* [29] *Are not two sparrows sold for a penny? Yet not one of them will fall to the ground apart from the will of your Father.* [30] *And even the very hairs of your head are all numbered.* [31] *So don't be afraid; you are worth more than many sparrows.'*
> (Matthew 10:27–31)

Emotional turmoil can twist the individual and damage the personality by influencing the choices he makes. Therefore Jesus emphasized how dangerous it was to live with the soulish realm dictating to the will. We are called by Him to lay *'psyche'* life down for a much better expression of life which we will call *'zoe life'*. *'Zoe life'* is the third type of expression of life that Jesus used in order to highlight what dominated the will of a man. *'Zoe'* is often used by Jesus along with the word *'eternal'* to indicate the kind of life Jesus gives us in place of the one we once had.

> *'For God so loved the world that he gave his one and only Son, that whoever believes in him shall not perish but have eternal life* (zoe).*'*
> (John 3:16)

'Zoe life' is the expression of life by which the will is seated in the spiritual perspective. It is the kind of lifestyle that is governed not by our emotions or the basic fleshly

needs that we have, but by the Spirit of God who has awakened our spirit to God.

> *'because through Christ Jesus the law of the Spirit of life* (zoe) *set me free from the law of sin and death.'*
> (Romans 8:2)

For the believer this eternal life springs from Jesus' death and resurrection on the cross. Because we have obeyed Him by going through the waters of baptism the old self is dead and buried.

> *'Or don't you know that all of us who were baptized into Christ Jesus were baptized into his death?* [4] *We were therefore buried with him through baptism into death in order that, just as Christ was raised from the dead through the glory of the Father, we too may live a new life* (zoe). [5] *If we have been united with him like this in his death, we will certainly also be united with him in his resurrection.* [6] *For we know that our old self was crucified with him so that the body of sin might be done away with, that we should no longer be slaves to sin –* [7] *because anyone who has died has been freed from sin.* [8] *Now if we died with Christ, we believe that we will also live with him.* [9] *For we know that since Christ was raised from the dead, he cannot die again; death no longer has mastery over him.* [10] *The death he died, he died to sin once for all; but the life he lives, he lives to God.* [11] *In the same way, count yourselves dead to sin but alive* (zoe) *to God in Christ Jesus.'* (Romans 6:3–11)

The binds and inhibitions of the old sinful personality have been crucified and buried with Christ. We are no longer bound by the carnal nature or the soulish nature. Rather we have entered into resurrection life with Jesus (Romans 6:5). This process of salvation will culminate in receiving a resurrection body in glory. We have already died and our whole attitude should be to count ourselves dead to our old carnal or soulish life but recognise that we are now spiritually alive to God in Christ Jesus (Romans 6:11). The consequences of having this eternal life as opposed to the old one is that the destructive aspects of personality have been dealt with on the cross.

> *'the sinful mind is hostile to God. It does not submit to God's law, nor can it do so. [8] Those controlled by the sinful nature cannot please God. [9] You, however, are controlled not by the sinful nature but by the Spirit, if the Spirit of God lives in you. And if anyone does not have the Spirit of Christ, he does not belong to Christ. [10] But if Christ is in you, your body is dead because of sin, yet your spirit is alive* (zoe) *because of righteousness. [11] And if the Spirit of him who raised Jesus from the dead is living* (zoe) *in you, he who raised Christ from the dead will also give life to your mortal bodies through his Spirit, who lives in you.* (Romans 8:7–11)

Now even our un-resurrected bodies are influenced by this new life of the Spirit. The principle of death is no longer at work in the personality but rather the law of the spirit of **'Zoe life'**. We can go back to the old soulish or carnal kind of life we used to live if we want to but it is not recommended.

> *'The one who sows to please his sinful nature, from that nature will reap destruction; the one who sows to please the Spirit, from the Spirit will reap eternal life.'*
> (Galatians 6:8)

Like Paul we can live in newness of life and liberty of expression of this new life by saying *'I no longer live but Christ lives* (zoe) *in me'*. Our personalities can be so transformed by the Spirit so that we can actually say with integrity, *'it is not I that lives but Christ in me'*.

> '*I have been crucified with Christ and I no longer live, but Christ lives* (zoe) *in me. The life I live in the body, I live by faith in the Son of God, who loved me and gave himself for me.*'
> (Galatians 2:20)

And so the believer is called to allow his whole personality to be transformed and conform to the image of Christ. Now, as we have seen here, if we are to effectively represent the image of Christ then there must be a transition from physical and soulish expression of life to a spiritual one.

When a parent gives birth to a child the child carries on the image of the parent. This is one means by which the image is carried on but also the child begins to copy the parents. **'People are made with the capacity for reproducing after their own image'**. This principle that God has written into relationships should not be surprising as God Himself reproduces after His own image.

> '*Then God said, "Let us make man in our image, in our likeness, and let them rule over the fish of the sea and the birds of the air, over the livestock, over all the earth, and over all the creatures that move along the ground."*'
> (Genesis 1:26)

We have been **'born again'** into a new family, recreated in the image of Christ. We have been set free from the control of sin and are now free to seat our will in the spiritual realm and thus express the attitude, nature and life of Christ. But to get there we must understand that the steps to a radically changed personality are progressive. To enhance our personality for God we must adopt an attitude similar to John the Baptist, who said *'I must decrease and he must increase'*. Our expressed personality, as we have learned, is an expression of all the things that *have maintained an 'influence'* on us. It is seen expressed in our habitual behaviour. John the Baptist chose to become less prominent as Christ grew more prominent and we should chose the same but recognise that it takes time.

Barriers to an Enhanced Personality

1. *The past*

To take the radical step of faith to an enhanced personality we will have to face the main impediments to change. People are resistant to change. We don't like things to radically alter if we can help it. Some would rather cleave to the secure past, regardless of the pain, hurt or difficulties arising out of that past. Due to a fear of change they cling to the security of the present circumstances regardless of how damaging they may be to them rather than take the steps of faith that they have to take. Some reasons for such strong attachment to the past include:

(a) Unhelpful counselling

Graham was a man that I met who had lived quite a horrific past. Having gone though what he called several sessions of inner healing and deliverance, he still felt that he needed much more. I chatted with him and sought to encourage him to recognise that the key to inner healing is to forgive those who have hurt you and repent of those you have hurt. But he was adamant that he needed deliverance to be able to get rid of some of these inner hurts. It appeared to me that he was actually afraid of the responsibility of living in freedom with respect to his past hurts. He had to hang on to a lifestyle within which he could blame his past for his present shortcomings. Many Christians today need to grow up with respect to their attitude about their past hurts. It is a trend that is noticeable in some Charismatic circles and thus needs to be addressed. Some inner healing that goes on is a syncretism of Christianity and psychological techniques. I once heard an horrific account of how one young lady had been counselled by an individual who was unbalanced about inner healing. The lady who had been raped was encouraged to recall the event in graphic detail and then was told to visualise Jesus being there and imagine Him putting back on articles of her underwear. When she told me all this I was shocked. I thought it was distasteful and disgusting. A lady who heard of the incident responded by saying *'I would have wondered why he did not stop it from happening if he was standing there.'*

(b) Manipulative

Not only can inner healing techniques encourage a lot of Christians to hold on to their past and to blame their past for their present state, it can also encourage Christians to cling to their human counsellor, producing highly dependant and suggestible individuals. I have come across many situations where a large percentage of people were under the influence of one individual and would listen to that person first before they listened to their elders. In one case most of them had gone through some sort of inner healing experience with that person. I believe that God wants to heal our emotions and set us free from inner hurts but I have witnessed to the fact that inner healing can become a hinderance to enhancing the personality where the individual lives in perpetual need for it as a means of lasting out the week until the next bout of deliverance. Though deliverance and healing from past hurts are important, dependency on them can become a hinderance to an enhanced personality.

(c) Past artifacts

Past sentimental artifacts can be a hinderance to enhancing your personality for God. Hindering artifacts can range from photographs to the very house we live in. After I had become a Christian I discovered that I had photographs of myself at parties and events which were basically trophies of past ungodly achievements; sinful episodes in my life of which I realised I was proud. The only recourse was to get rid of them and bury the past. How could my personality be enhanced for God if I was holding on to ungodly memories of a sinful past that ought to have been buried at baptism? Getting rid of the photographs in repentance was the only thing to do. Some individuals need to let go of a lot more than just old photographs. I have been amazed to find a definite sentimental attachment to idols of Buddha, Hinduism etc. in some homes.

2. The demands of the future

It dawned on me that clinging to the past was a pattern that seems to repeat itself over and over again because *'familiarity spells security, comfort and stability'*. Human beings like the familiar and the non-threatening. That is why we hate war and love peace. We put security locks on our windows and doors because we hate anything threatening. The demands of change can appear daunting and greatly demanding, consequently change can appear as a demerit regardless of its virtues. Fear is a wall that must be shattered if we are going to enhance our personality.

3. Strong relationships

People at times are the reason why we have not yet gone on with God. It can be very difficult to admit this and let go because we somehow equate letting go of a loved one as rejecting them. But this is not the case. Letting go means no longer depending on that relationship in an unhealthy way. People will put others before Christ in an unhealthy way and may not even realise that they are doing it or that it means that our family or friends have a greater pull and thus more important place in our life. One notes from this that *'the stronger the emotional attachment the greater the personal involvement'*. Individuals that are emotionally attached to something or someone will get personally involved with that person or thing. Take fishing for example. I would never consider sitting in a boat with a fishing rod for hours on end hoping to catch a fish. It does nothing for me emotionally. I might consider having a go at the event but I would not chose to spend my time in the middle of a lake fishing. Others though would jump at the chance. Mention the word 'fish' to some people and they are off, recounting amazing near catches and wonderful fishing spots they have personally been to. Again this proves *'the stronger the emotional attachment the greater the personal involvement'*.

The Mirror of the Personality

In relationships between two people the same is true. I have several friends but emotionally I have a greater personal involvement with my wife than with my friends. Most people find this an acceptable state of affairs but the minute I mention the fact that Jesus is more important to me than my wife, some people cannot cope with it. Why? It is only because they are not as strongly emotionally attached to Jesus as they ought to be and so are not as personally involved with Him as they should be. If that is the case for you the solution is to repent of your sins and commit your life to Christ in the way He requires it. You do this by firstly becoming born again. If you are not born again, turn to the back of this book at this point and read the Appendix. If you are born again but have not been putting Him first the journey to an enhancement of personality begins at the cross of Jesus Christ. Repent of not putting Him first. I have found that by putting Jesus first in my life I can actually love my wife better than I would have if I had put her first. One of the wonderful statements that my wife makes is *'when at times I would not think of putting things right with Yinka purely because I love him, I will put things right with him because I love Jesus'*.

Now that we have looked at how personality is shaped by the choices we make and influenced by where we allow the will to find its seat of government in our lives, we have the key to change our personalities as encouraged in the word of God.

Chapter 3

Purposeful Personalities

Man has to interact with his environment because of his needs and within that environment he expresses himself. We could classify the things that provoke interaction with our environment into four categories of needs.

The first category is the constraint of a man's spirit. Because we are created spiritual beings we search for spiritual fulfilment. If a man cannot find his way to God he will seek to meet his spirit's needs by giving worship to something else. This could range from worshipping himself and the things he has created, to worshipping the demons behind idols, nature worship or even the demons which communicate to people pretending to be deceased loved ones. Man interacts with his environment seeking to meet the needs of his spirit. The second category of needs springs from man's emotional requirements such as the need for companionship. Loneliness, as we have seen, is not a state that God considers helpful to man's well-being. Until this day, just like Adam, we seek to interact with our environment in order that we might find friends and a companion to share our life with. The third category of necessities which causes man to interact with his environment is his physical requirements. Hunger causes man to plant, sow and reap and the need for physical shelter causes him to dig, build and erect homes.

The fourth category which we will look at in detail at this point is his purpose in life. God wrote into man the need for work. Having made Adam, God then set him to work in the Garden. Even Eve was created with the intention that one of her prime purposes was to be a help mate to Adam. Before we go any further it is important to realise that the best way of fulfilling our purpose is to have a heart similar to John the Baptist. Like him we must be willing to decrease while Christ increases. If we are not going to fulfil God's purpose but rather pursue selfish and self-centred purposes then we will not be enhancing our personality for God. Jesus said a man can only serve one master. The same is true about our purpose in life; we will either be serving our purpose or God's.

Purpose is a Part of Your Identity

Our identity is that which is ours by birth. The minute we are born we are given a name which identifies us. We are known as belonging to a particular family and by our name are identifiable. The minute the House of Windsor is mentioned the hearers realise that it is the royal family that is being mentioned. Other things that identify an individual are his character, attitude and mannerisms. This is why an impersonator can stand up on the stage, make a few funny faces and we instantly recognise the star or public figure they are impersonating. In simple terms *'identity is that by which a person is known'*. And so when someone mentions the Saviour of the world we immediately identify that individual as Jesus. His other names, The Lamb of God, Prince of Peace and The Healer all immediately identify Jesus. Most of His names remind us of **what He did** and still does today. We are able to identify who is being spoken of because of what He did. The mention of Moses further proves the point. What image is conjured up for many people when his name is mentioned? Most people, when asked to share what their first thought is at the mention of Moses' name, respond by saying the Red Sea or the Ten Commandments. It is virtually impossible to consider Moses without considering what he did; it is part of his identity. Moses was a man who fulfilled the purpose for which he was created. Moses was made with a purpose in mind. This is a principle in creation *'everything is made for a purpose'*. The sun created by God provides light by which we see, and it provides light by which plants can grow. A chair made by a man is meant to seat individuals and give them rest, a car is made for the purpose of transportation. Even man is made for a purpose and Adam's was initially to be God's friend and gardener. Purpose, then, is the framework and context for man's expression of his personality, because God made us for a purpose. Obviously the ultimate purpose of our creation was to be God's children, but He also created us with other roles in mind. All this helps us to understand why our work or job in life is always so important to us. When the revelation that what we do is an extension or expression of our personality dawns on us we can better understand and cope with the pressures associated with our work or call. Like Jesus, our identity is wrapped up in what we do, and what we do is part of our personality. Jesus is The Light of The World. He brings light to man's darkened heart, and thus His work is wrapped up in His person, it is part of everything that He is, part of His personality because the light of the world brings light to the world (John 8:12). Understanding this helps us understand ourselves. No psychologist or worldly system which tries to understand man could ever discover this because it is revelation that springs forth from a study of God's word and not man's interpretation of man.

(a) Therefore purpose matters as much as identity

It is often wrongly emphasised in Christian circles that the only thing that matters is who we are in Christ, not what we can do. I have witnessed times when an individual who has failed to achieve something he set out on despite his enthusiasm has been told that the results of his efforts do not matter, because it is who he is in Christ that matters. Michael is one individual who was so advised. He believed that he should be an evangelist, but having raised people's interest in the Gospel he never seemed able to bring his efforts to fruition by leading those interested through to the Lord. There was no doubt that he had the zeal but he did not yet have the experience. He was counselled not to worry and was told 'who you are in Christ is more important than what you can do, so do not worry about the results'. This is an example of bad counselling. The results definitely matter. If not to the counsellor it certainly matters to the counselled individual. The desire and zeal to preach the Gospel, or anything else we feel God wants us to do, is always to be encouraged and the results we achieve should matter dearly to us. **'Everybody wants to produce good results from their hard labour'**. The best advice to Michael would have been 'get alongside someone with a proven ministry in evangelism in the church and find out from them how to bring a person right through'. When people say 'who we are in Christ is what is important not what we can do' I understand that the motivation is often to placate feelings of inadequacy or failure, but I disagree with the statement when it is used as an excuse. What we do, or rather what we are created to do, is as important as who we are in Christ. We will face problems when we try to do things we were not created to do, things we have not given the Lord a chance to train us up in, or things God has not called us to do. Even when we are told it does not matter what we do, inwardly we long to do something that brings glory to God and causes us to feel fulfilled in our life. What Jesus did matters. He is not important only because He is the Christ but also by virtue of what He did. From eternity it was purposed that He should die for us (Ephesians 1:4).

(b) Drive helps us achieve our purpose

The longing to achieve that people have is sometimes called *'drive'* and was given to us by God. It was He that put a dimension of desire into our emotions which produces drive. **'The strength to which our desires motivate us is the strength to which our drive motivates us'**. Drive motivates us to achieve our purpose in life. Some think it is wrong for a Christian to have ambitions but this cannot be. Jesus

Himself had a goal which He set out to accomplish. He stuck at it until He was able to say 'it is finished' on the cross. He achieved what He set out for. The only time ambition becomes a problem is when it does not arise out of what God is saying to us or directing us in. Drive manifests itself in ambition. How can it be wrong to have drive if God, in whose image we are made, has drive? God intends, purposes, plans and wills in order that His purposes might prevail. He is a determined God who exercises His sovereignty resolutely until His will comes to pass. It is not surprising we reflect this aspect of God. When we realise that in Christ Jesus we have been created for the purpose of good works then it helps us to understand where godly zeal and ambitions come from, because when we walk closely to the Lord we want to please Him.

> *'For we are God's workmanship, created in Christ Jesus to do good works, which God prepared in advance for us to do.'* (Ephesians 2:10)

God has specific works for each one of us, but we have a part to play in discovering these works. **'As believers *the degree to which we fulfil God's purpose in our lives is the degree to which we will feel fulfilled in our personality'*.** Jesus was joy-filled at the prospect of fulfilling the purpose for which He came (Hebrews 12:2). Each one of us also has a role to fulfil which is on God's agenda. ***'The degree to which we walk with God is the degree to which we will fulfil the purpose for which we were created'***. We need to take the time to find out from God what He would have us do with our lives and not simply get excited about what we could do for God. Another word for drive is zeal. Zeal or drive is not an excuse for making mistakes. Zeal is only good when based on adequate knowledge of what the Lord desires (Proverbs 19:2). When drive is based on adequate knowledge we can call it *'Godly ambition'*. This is a God centred and considered approach to strong desires which can be at work within us. Ambition is okay as long as it is initiated by and springs forth from God's Spirit. If it is from the Holy Spirit then it needs to be admitted. Every ambition Jesus had was brought to Him by the Holy Spirit and He would do nothing except what God wanted Him to do. In this Jesus was zealous and determined and so endured everything in order to accomplish His objective. We are encouraged to copy this example.

> *'Let us fix our eyes on Jesus, the author and perfecter of our faith, who for the joy set before him endured the cross, scorning its shame, and sat down at the right hand of the throne of God.'* (Hebrews 12:2)

(c) Drive makes use of our potential

'Everything God has made possesses potential'. Coal, for instance, has the potential to be a source of heat. Water not only refreshes when it is drunk, it also has the potential to be used to put fires out and drive trains. Men can make use of the things God has created and derive benefit from them as God's creation is full of potential. A car has tremendous potential energy stored up in the petrol, but, until the key is turned the plugs do not fire, the pistons stand still and the potential energy is not utilised. Drive is like the key that turns the engine on and when it is submitted to the Holy Spirit that potential that each of us has becomes infinite in the hands of the Spirit of God whose power is infinite. If someone other than the owner of the car takes it on a joyride then the petrol will be used up and all that potential energy will be wasted. If desires other than Godly ones take a hold of our lives we could end up wasting the potential that God has given to us (Ephesians 2:10). Bezaleel son of Uri was a gifted man, but God made it clear that it was He who placed the special giftings within him for His special purposes.

> *'See, I have called by name Bezaleel the son of Uri, the son of Hur, of the tribe of Judah:* [3] *And I have filled him with the spirit of God, in wisdom, and in understanding,*

and in knowledge, and in all manner of workmanship, ^{4} To devise cunning works, to work in gold, and in silver, and in brass.' (Exodus 31:2–4 KJV)

On the basis of Ephesians 2:10 we ought to confess out loud that we have a purpose in this life and feed this belief and confession so that it has the energy to function. *'Everything needs energy to function'*. A plant can not grow unless it gets energy from the sun; a plane can not fly unless it has fuel. Drive feeds on what it is fed, because *'drive needs energy to function'* and then *'drive makes use of our potential'*. If godly ambition is dampened it could put out the drive. Drive which springs forth from our desire to please God needs to be fed not dampened. But if we allow sin to energise or give birth to our drive then it will lead to death.

'But every man is tempted, when he is drawn away of his own lust, and enticed. ^{15} Then when lust hath conceived, it bringeth forth sin: and sin, when it is finished, bringeth forth death.' (James 1:14–15 KJV)

Going back to the example of a car *'the wrong driver will take you in the wrong direction'*. If greed, malice or envy get into the driving seat then we will end up going in a different direction to the one God desires.The good news is, we can derive an understanding of our potential and how to use our gifting from God's word, in order that we might be able to do these good works that God has for us to do.

'All scripture is given by inspiration of God, and is profitable for doctrine, for reproof, for correction, for instruction in righteousness: ^{17} That the man of God may be perfect, thoroughly furnished unto all good works.' (2 Timothy 3:16–17 KJV)

One way of feeding Godly ambition is to provoke one another into doing good works and fulfilling the purpose for which we were created (Hebrews 10:24). We also should remind each other that letting go of trust in God or a good conscience can shipwreck our faith and limit our potential.

> *'Holding faith, and a good conscience; which some having put away concerning faith have made shipwreck.'*
> (1 Timothy 1:19 KJV)

If a desire other than a godly one gets into the driving seat of our hearts then we could end up wasting our energy and shipwrecking our potential in God.

(d) Meaningful purpose is the desire of all

When was the last time you met someone who passionately dreamed of becoming a tramp? ***'Everyone dreams of a meaningful purpose in life'***. While not wanting to degrade tramps and recognising that God loves tramps as much as He loves anybody else, it is clear that we all dream of achieving. From childhood we all dream of doing something worthwhile with our lives. Dreams by nature tend to be filled with a hope of achievement and the accomplishment of things that command respect. We dream of standing out by doing something unique and worthy of the Lord.

> *'For this reason, since the day we heard about you, we have not stopped praying for you and asking God to fill you with the knowledge of his will through all spiritual wisdom and understanding. [10] And we pray this in order that you may live a life worthy of the Lord and may please him in every way: bearing fruit in every good work, growing in the knowledge of God.'*
> (Colossians 1:9–10)

Paul prayed that the believers at Colosse would stand out. We know instinctively that aiming for something meaningful in life will stretch us, and, we realise that it will produce some strains, but nevertheless we still dream of accomplishing something special and unique. God uses the imaginative aspect of man to encourage him forwards and onwards, by planting desires and dreams into a man's heart.

> *'The king's heart is in the hand of the LORD; he directs it like a watercourse wherever he pleases.'*
> (Proverbs 21:1)

In Deuteronomy chapter 28 He gave a general list of blessings and curses to the whole of His people. He encouraged them to think of their future in terms of health, prosperity and productiveness if they obeyed. They did not know exactly what awaited them in the future but they were encouraged to think of it in terms of peace and prosperity. He also gave specific hopes and dreams to specific individuals. Abraham was one such individual that was given much to hope for by God. Lot and he had both decided to part company because their herds had grown too big to stay together. Lot chose to go east because of the fertility of the land. But immediately God told Abraham that he had a different agenda and told him to look at the whole of the land. All of it would be his and his descendants'. God enlarged his dreams and vision. Simeon the Jew was another who dreamed. He dreamed of seeing the Messiah. Having read the word of God and understood the prophecy of His coming, the scriptures produced a desire to see the Lord.

> *'Now there was a man in Jerusalem called Simeon, who was righteous and devout. He was waiting for the consolation of Israel, and the Holy Spirit was upon him.* [26] *It had been revealed to him by the Holy Spirit that he would not die before he had seen the Lord's Christ.* [27] *Moved by the Spirit, he went into the temple courts. When the parents brought in the child Jesus to do for him what the custom of the Law required,* [28] *Simeon took him in his arms and praised God, saying:* [29] *"Sovereign Lord, as you have promised, you now dismiss your servant in peace.* [30] *For my eyes have seen your salvation."'*
> (Luke 2:24–30)

Dreams should arise out of what God has said. If they do not then we can have no confidence in their fulfilment or worth.

Discovering Our Purpose

Achieving even the smallest of goals is rewarding, but where the achievement is particularly noteworthy we win the respect of others and are left with feelings of immense satisfaction. We were chosen to bear good fruit and to be fruitful, thus we will naturally achieve things in God. Achievement that comes through obeying God feeds a right kind of boldness, confidence, adventurousness and it contributes to personal growth. It also encourages our drive. Many struggle with discovering God's purpose for their life. The struggle is often painful as individuals try very hard to find the purpose for which they were created. The first step we must take in order to discover our purpose is to become clear about, and to understand what we are founding our lives upon. I believe that before we ask ourselves 'what is God's purpose for my life?' we need to ask the question: What are the basic foundations upon which I am building right now? This is ascertained when we look at our convictions. Knowing this is vital because *'the convictions by which you live reveal the purpose for which you live'*. A comparison of two kings helps us to see this point. Herod lived to be king; this was the overriding drive in his heart. When he heard that there might be a rival king he ordered the death of all children under the age of two years. His convictions revealed the purpose for which he lived. He always had to be number one. He founded his life on his own goals and his desires. King David, however, lived to praise God, and, when the opportunity came for him to kill his rival King Saul he chose not to, saying he would not touch the Lord's anointed. Again his convictions revealed the purpose for which he was living. God was number one in his life not the throne.

Caleb was a man who ultimately fulfilled God's purpose for his life. He had been one of the twelve spies who had

Purposeful Personalities

been sent from Kadesh Barnea to explore the land that the Lord had promised them. Only he and Joshua came back with a report that considered the word of the LORD a better foundation to build upon and did not consider the fear of the giants a good foundation from which to proceed into the promised land. He said his report was according to his convictions. Forty years later after they had entered the promised land Caleb laid claim to God's promise to give him an inheritance in the Land. The city he eventually took and conquered Kiriath Arba (later known as Hebron) was founded by Arba the patriarch amongst the Anakites, a race of giants. Caleb's convictions affected the purpose for which he lived and *'convictions always affect the purpose for which a man lives'*. Samson unfortunately did not hold his professed convictions as a Jew with any strength. He would never be conquered as long as he kept the source of his strength secret. Samson was being raised up by God to be a deliverer amongst his people but unfortunately he slept around (Judges 16:1–4; 14–15) and this led to his downfall. He did not value God's word to him and sold his inheritance for peace confessing to Delilah the secret of his strength (Judges 16:16–17). It ended up with him in chains and captured by his Palestinian enemies. His purpose in life was cut short because he ended up spending years in shameful captivity at the hands of his peoples' enemies. His convictions ended up affecting his purpose. He won some skirmishes but never really won any major battles.

What we learn from these examples is *'if you don't settle your convictions your convictions will settle your purpose'*. A conviction is that which convinces you. They are the foundations upon which you build your life or boundary lines by which you regulate your walk in life. They are not necessarily moral but can hold, for example, a moral, spiritual or academic context. Foundational convictions are thus important: we need to settle them before they settle us.

I remember listening to a famous preacher speaking at a family service. He said something which I found interesting and educational. Whatever problems he and his wife might face, they never put their relationship on the line. Whatever the difficulties, they had made up their mind that the relationship would never be threatened. I have since applied this principle to many other aspects of my life concerning the word of God because I have come to realise that though it is true to state as I did in chapter one, that *'attractiveness is the means by which relationships are initiated'*, this is not enough. We also need to acknowledge that *'agreement is the means by which relationships are maintained'*. Our convictions are vital if we are to walk in close fellowship with God. The very covenant in which we stand in relationship with God is an agreement. To have an unbroken relationship with the Lord we need to make up our minds and determine that we will never put our relationship with God on the line. If we want our personalities enhanced for God then we will cleave to covenant requirements. Most of us have made up our mind that we would never murder anybody whatever the justification. But, some have not made up their minds that lying is bad whatever the circumstances. We need to settle our convictions about these issues from the word of God. Satan, and often more probably other people, or at times our circumstances, will test our convictions by putting pressure on us or providing us with opportunities through which we could sin. But we can overcome both Satan and the circumstances by making our mind up not to disobey God before we are tempted in difficult circumstances.

> *'They overcame him by the blood of the Lamb and by the word of their testimony; they did not love their lives so much as to shrink from death.'* (Revelation 12:11)

Another key in discovering God's purpose for our life is coming to the realisation that God always moves us on in steps which are never final but progressive until we reach perfection in glory. There is no cut-off point at which we suddenly begin to live in God's purpose for our life. Rather every day should be another step in His purposes. Many want to fulfil God's specific call upon their life but if we are to fulfil the specific we must first fulfil His general purposes. His general purposes are not hard to understand or difficult to find. They are written all over the pages of Scripture. If you want to know His specific purposes for your life why not start with a firm commitment to some general ones like love, faith, repentance from dead works and commitment to church?

> *'Let us hold unswervingly to the hope we profess, for he who promised is faithful. *[24]* And let us consider how we may spur one another on toward love and good deeds. *[25]* Let us not give up meeting together, as some are in the habit of doing, but let us encourage one another – and all the more as you see the Day approaching. *[26]* If we deliberately keep on sinning after we have received the knowledge of the truth, no sacrifice for sins is left.'*
> (Hebrews 10:23–26)

If we are not willing to walk in the general will of God why bother about the specific? If we are not even going to bother trying to fulfil the general, what makes us think we are going to fulfil the specific? Caleb fulfilled God's general will and so fulfilled God's specific. Jesus spent thirty years fulfilling the general will of God and so was able to fulfil the specific. **'Fulfilment of the specific comes out of fulfilment of the general'** as surely as he who is faithful in the little things will be faithful with much. We can be confident that if generally we are obeying God then we cannot miss His will for our lives, for the steps of a righteous man are ordered by God. The Lord's specific call will come and when it does you cannot miss it. You can ignore it, deny it or even reject it but you can not miss it. I have spent a lot of time with people who felt a call from God ten, twenty, sometimes thirty years ago, but because of one circumstance or another did not respond to the call. They did not miss the call. They simply did nothing about it or were bound up by circumstances and so did not pursue the call.

Another important key that will help us not to miss God's

purpose for our life is to make ourselves accountable in our call. When Adam was put in the garden he was not left without instruction. His task was to care for Eden (Genesis 2:15). His was the tenancy of the earth but the garden was God's and Adam was *'accountable'* to God for what he did in the garden and so when he stepped over the boundary line by eating the fruit he was ushered out of the garden. Today God gives us the opportunity to be accountable in the church. It is a pattern seen throughout the whole of scripture. **'Wherever God gives responsibility He always calls for accountability'**. King David was called to account for the death of Uriah, Saul was called to account for plundering the spoils from the battle against the Amalekites, Adam and Eve were called to account for eating of the tree, in fact the whole world will be called to account for its sin. Because God is the one who has given us our life, He will demand an accounting for how we have lived. And so in the church we ought to be accountable to those God has placed over us. The trouble is that in today's society accountability and responsibility are almost dirty words, especially within the church because of the abuse or excess of some leaders in using their positions of responsibility. Some leaders have strayed over into heavy shepherding, a topic I have extensively covered in my book *Manipulation Domination and Control*, and thus some leaders have put many Christians off the idea of being accountable. Consequentially for many the important consideration is freedom that excludes any kind of accountability. I do not believe that this is scriptural. If we are going to fulfil God's purpose for our lives we need the help that comes in the form of accountability within the context of local church, missionary organisation or group of believers dedicated to such a call as we may be given by God.

This accountability becomes genuine when you admit to your church leaders and friends what you think your call in life is even if you are not sure about it. Friends and church leaders will either help us see that we are being unrealistic, or encourage us to allow God to train us and get us ready for those things we have openly confessed to as works God wants us to do. Openly confessing makes us vulnerable, but it also means that we are more likely to achieve our purpose in life. This is because a good leader or good friend will not allow us to waste our potential in life and then say twenty years later 'well, I thought you should have tried such and such'. No; a good leader or a good friend will provoke you to do something about what you believe is the call of God on your life. Remember that problems arise because,

(1) We try to do things God never intended us to do.
(2) We try to do things we have not given the Lord a chance to train us up in.
(3) We do not settle our foundational convictions.
(4) We do not admit what we believe to be the call of God upon our lives.

PART B:

How to Enhance Your Personality

Chapter 4

Redirecting, Reseating and Anchoring Our Will and Emotions

As we have seen the will is only as powerful as that which exerts the most force on it. Consequently it is important to ensure that our will is seated in, or governed by the spirit and not the soul. As we learned in the last chapter personality is that which we have learned to express by choice, and so *'if our will is controlled by the Holy Spirit rather than the soul we can enhance our personalities for God'*.

But how do we make sure that the spirit is the overriding principle in our lives rather than the soul? In the face of great emotional stress and difficulties many Christians struggle with this issue. Living *'zoe life'* or spiritually dominated and controlled life is desired by many but how do we achieve it?

(a) Jesus Reseated His Will and Emotions

Jesus is the best example of one who walked in the Spirit. How did He cope with His emotions? Because He was fully man we should be able to discover from Him the perfect means of controlling our emotions. The secret of channelling our emotional energy appears to be found in the dramatic episode that unfolds in the gospel of Mark. Here the scripture records that Jesus was overwhelmed by His emotions.

'They went to a place called Gethsemane, and Jesus said to his disciples, "Sit here while I pray." [33] *He took Peter, James and John along with him, and he began to be deeply distressed and troubled.* [34] ***"My soul is overwhelmed with sorrow to the point of death,"*** *he said to them.* ***"Stay here and keep watch."*** [35] *Going a little farther, he fell to the ground and prayed that if possible the hour might pass from him.* [36] *"Abba, Father," he said, "everything is possible for you. Take this cup from me. Yet not what I will, but what you will."* [37] *Then he returned to his disciples and found them sleeping. "Simon," he said to Peter, "are you asleep? Could you not keep watch for one hour?* [38] *Watch and pray so that you will not fall into temptation. The spirit is willing, but the body is weak."* [39] *Once more he went away and prayed the same thing.* [40] *When he came back, he again found them sleeping, because their eyes were heavy. They did not know what to say to him.* [41] *Returning the third time, he said to them, "Are you still sleeping and resting? Enough! The hour has come. Look, the Son of Man is betrayed into the hands of sinners."'* (Mark 14:32–41)

Jesus was completely overwhelmed by His emotions, we are told. There are several interesting things that this episode of Jesus' life teaches us about emotions. Firstly *'emotions have a focal point'*. A lot of people only ever pray when they are in trouble because when they reach the end of their resources they begin to change their focus and gaze upwards towards God. Many a person having been shipwrecked at sea has eventually turned to prayer after gazing into the horizon and losing hope that they would be rescued. They have turned to God and pleaded for His intervention in a drastic situation. Emotionally everyone needs a focal point, something or someone to lean on in a difficult situation. Jesus, being deeply distressed and emotionally overwhelmed, fixed His gaze steadily upon God refusing to look elsewhere until He could finally lay down His own will. The key to Him overcoming in this difficult time was that He did

Redirecting, Reseating and Anchoring Our Will and Emotions

not stop praying until He came to a place of emotional rest. Contrast the response of His disciples in the same situation. They were also emotionally disturbed, they knew that Jesus' coming to Jerusalem meant trouble; He had explained this to them earlier.

> *'From that time on Jesus began to explain to his disciples that he must go to Jerusalem and suffer many things at the hands of the elders, chief priests and teachers of the law, and that he must be killed and on the third day be raised to life.'* (Matthew 16:21)

They also knew (hence it was recorded) that Jesus Himself was troubled. But there is a contrast in the way they responded when we compare it to the way Jesus responded. I don't believe that they were just physically tired. It appears that they had the kind of tiredness that comes from personal desperation. When an individual is in distress it can bring on a fainting feeling on the inside or feelings of tiredness, sluggishness and worry. The disciples were trying to suppress their emotions by sleeping. Suppressed emotions can eventually lead to all kinds of physical and mental illnesses if they are not brought to God. One of the things Jesus was trying to teach His disciples on the night He was betrayed was how to channel their distress and lack of hope by showing them how He channelled His emotions. Worry and sleep were not the answer but rather a seeking after the face of God. **'Worry touches the emotions, prayer touches God'**. Unfortunately a lot of people confuse worry with prayer. They at times confuse the act of thinking a lot about a problem with actually coming to a place of intimacy with God in prayer. **'Redirecting the soul in prayer conquers all our fears'**. Over and over again the psalmist confesses this (Psalm 141:8). Daniel put his trust in the Lord and prayed even when told not to, despite the consequences he knew he would have to face. He was not afraid of the repercussion of fellowshiping with God; he put his hope in God and so when he was thrown in the lions den he was not afraid. And in the

Garden Jesus put His hope in God regardless of the strong emotional turmoil He went through. This is not the only time that Jesus had taught them the importance of prayer as a means of communing with God. The disciples recognised Jesus' prayer life as the powerhouse of His ministry and so asked Him to teach them how to pray (Luke 11:1-5). In what has affectionately come to be known as the Lord's prayer He taught them that *'the focus of prayer is God not needs'* (Luke 11:2). Needs are important but relationship with God must come first. It is clear that *'people that talk to each other can walk with each other'*. Any breakdown in communication eventually will lead to a breakdown in relationship. When a husband and wife go through a time of difficulty, if they fail to communicate it can lead to a breakdown in the marriage. In the middle of great emotional distress Jesus was still concerned with teaching them in the garden of Gethsemane that focusing on God, not their emotional problems, was what they ought to be doing. In Luke's account of the Lord's prayer, Jesus went on to teach that persistence in prayer results in us receiving more of the Holy Spirit.

> *'So I say to you: Ask and it will be given to you; seek and you will find; knock and the door will be opened to you. ^{10} For everyone who asks receives; he who seeks finds; and to him who knocks, the door will be opened. ^{11} Which of you fathers, if your son asks for a fish, will give him a snake instead? ^{12} Or if he asks for an egg, will give him a scorpion? ^{13} If you then, though you are evil, know how to give good gifts to your children, how much more will your Father in heaven give the Holy Spirit to those who ask him!'* (Luke 11:9-13)

The Lord is saying here that whatever we ask for in prayer, the answer to our prayer must come from, and ultimately is, the Holy Spirit. Because that which is born of the flesh is flesh but that which is born of the spirit is spirit. I have noticed people copy Jesus' example and lay down their emotional problems without realizing it at camps and conferences. They go to a camp or conference with all kinds of emotional needs and problems and then find **a new lease** in their prayer and devotional life. They suddenly believe that they can obey God in areas that He has been challenging them about and they become prepared to do something about it. ***'Redirecting the emotions in prayer reseats our wills from the soulish to the spiritual'***. The transformation is incredible at times, but because they are in an atmosphere of praise, worship and the word, they can lay down their problems. Like Jesus in the garden they focus on God and let go of their difficulties. But unlike Jesus when they get home, instead of persisting they let go of their new lease. ***'The problem with any new lease is it is only a temporary state of affairs'***. If it is not nurtured, this new lease will fizzle out. New and existing encounters with God are good, but ongoing fellowship and persistence in prayer with Him is better.

> *'And pray in the Spirit on all occasions with all kinds of prayers and requests. With this in mind, be alert and always keep on praying for all the saints.'*
> (Ephesians 6:18)

The command to pray on all occasions is not a call to a momentary state. It is a call to the kind of persistence in prayer that receives more of the Spirit by which we have access to God. This is what I believe happens at many camps, and why so many have such a wonderful time and feel so great. They lay down their emotions, concentrate on God and receive more of the Holy Spirit. Consequently they find that it is easier to meet with God,

> *'For through him we both have access to the Father by one Spirit.'* (Ephesians 2:18)

But when people get back home from the various camps and conferences they suddenly find themselves back in their daily routine and having to face the emotional strains and problems they left behind. It is at this point that they need to do what Jesus did in the garden and redirect their emotions in a God-ward direction. They need to keep in step with the Spirit rather than succumbing to the soul. The conflicts between the soul and the spirit are never greater than when people leave the atmosphere of a camp or conference and go back home. Sometimes people confuse an emotional high as a spiritual high. This, as we have seen in chapter 2, is because the manifestation of the soul and the spirit are so alike that only the sword of the Spirit (i.e. the Bible) can differentiate between them.

> *'For the word of God is living and active. Sharper than any double-edged sword, it penetrates even to dividing soul and spirit, joints and marrow; it judges the thoughts and attitudes of the heart.'* (Hebrews 4:12)

(b) The Spirit Needs to be in Ascendancy

Until the Spirit is in ascendancy and the seat of our will is governed from the spirit, then our will must either be governed by the flesh or the soul. When we pray like Jesus prayed, despite and regardless of our difficult circumstances, it has the effect of allowing the Spirit to fill us. It is at this point that our personalities can be enhanced for God because our will can submit to God, as we find ourselves able to keep in step with the Spirit and ignore the wrong emotional desire and frustrations that hinder our walk. Our personalities can flow in the way God would be pleased with when our will is seated in the spirit and not in the soul.

When the will is reseated from the soul into the realm of the spirit then the simple and individual choices we make will change. As our choices change our habit patterns will change, hence our personalities will be transformed both consciously and subconsciously. This is what happens to many new converts and at times the transformation is amazing. It never ceases to bless me to see converts subconsciously stop bad language without realising it.

(c) Reseating the Will Helps Conquer Sin

Other benefits of redirecting and reseating the will from the soulish realm into the spiritual realm are that we will better be able to handle and resist sin. If we divide sin up into its three constituent parts, we will better understand why there is a greater ability to resist sin when the will is seated in the spirit. In Galatians chapter 5:16-21 we find sin's constituent parts clearly laid out.
(1) **Sins that affect the flesh**: sexual immorality, impurity and debauchery; orgies and drunkenness (verses 19 and 20).
(2) **Sins that affect the spirit of a man**: idolatry and witchcraft (verse 20).
(3) **Sins which affect the soul of a man**: hatred, discord, jealousy, fits of rage, selfish ambition, dissension, factions and envy (verse 20).

With the will seated in the spirit and the emotions focused on God, sins of the flesh or soul become less of a temptation and our personalities become more of a witness unto the name of Jesus. When the *'influence'* of the flesh and soul are not as strong as the *'influence'* of the spirit on my will, then they have less power to tempt me.

Some important lessons have to be learned from what happened to Jesus in the Garden. Firstly it is important to note that the soul can only ever be healed when we meet with God. I have met hardened criminals and even ex SAS servicemen who I can truly describe as pools of peace, people who have come out of difficult and violent situations and now having met God have become pools of peace. Having received Jesus' provision from the cross and fellowshiped with Him their lives and personalities have so changed that they no longer resemble the violent and hardened persons they were, but rather reflect the peace of God. *'If the soul is to be healed from past hurts and horrific traumas and memories then there needs to be an encounter with God' 'Human comfort is good and can be timely but divine comfort is perfect and lasts for eternity'.* Friends can comfort for a season but God can comfort for ever. Prayer brings us face to face with God's love and enables us to rest in peace. Another important but wonderful aspect of coming to God in prayer is that we learn more from God Himself.

> *'Come to me, all you who are weary and burdened, and I will give you rest. [29] Take my yoke upon you and learn from me, for I am gentle and humble in heart, and you will find rest for your souls. [30] For my yoke is easy and my burden is light.'* (Matthew 11:28–30)

In coming to Christ in prayer our souls are taught and discipled by Christ. We find that in serving Him we can experience peace and rest that is far superior to anything the world could offer. The redirected soul, having learned from God, can walk in God's will.

(d) The Anchoring of the Soul

Having redirected our emotions and reseated our will, we need to anchor our souls. Many Christians I meet tend to have yo-yo existences, up on a high one week down on a low the next. Once we have redirected our emotions and reseated our will in the spirit, we can then anchor our souls by concentrating on aspects of the hope stored up for us.

> *'God did this so that, by two unchangeable things in which it is impossible for God to lie, we who have fled to take hold of the hope offered to us may be greatly encouraged.'* (Hebrews 6:18)

Hope is an emotional feeling and rational expectation. Scriptural hope brings our emotions into a place of stability. This is because scriptural hope is secure whilst worldly hope is unstable, worries and is doubtful that it will receive what is hoped for. This is the kind of hope that Herod had.

> *'When Herod saw Jesus, he was greatly pleased, because for a long time he had been wanting to see him. From what he had heard about him, he hoped to see him perform some miracle.'* (Luke 23:8)

Herod was disappointed because his hope was not based on the word of God. Scriptural hope is not doubt-filled but focuses its attention on God. It fills with eager expectations and arises because of what God's word says to us:

> *'For everything that was written in the past was written to teach us, so that through endurance and the encouragement of the Scriptures we might have hope.'*
> (Romans 15:4)

In fact this hope is found in us when we become saved (born again), having repented of our sins.

> *'For in this hope we were saved. But hope that is seen is no hope at all. Who hopes for what he already has?'*
> (Romans 8:24)

Our emotions become stable and anchored in this hope, and our faith is strengthened as a result of our illumination which arises from understanding this hope to which we are called. This is powerful and dynamic.

> *'I pray also that the eyes of your heart may be enlightened in order that you may know the hope to which he has called you, the riches of his glorious inheritance in the saints.'* (Ephesians 1:18)

The fact that this hope is different from worldly hope and that it is an anchor for the soul is seen in the way it affects our emotions when we lose loved ones. We do not grieve like unbelievers. The reason they grieve the way they do is because they have no genuine hope.

> *'Brothers, we do not want you to be ignorant about those who fall asleep, or to grieve like the rest of men, who have no hope.'* (1 Thessalonians 4:13)

Our emotions are no longer subject to wild swings because of dramatic events, rather we can be stable emotionally, and so are described as soaring on wings like eagles (Isaiah 40:31), and because of this stability we can produce and express the kind of faith and love that makes us attractive people.

> *'because we have heard of your faith in Christ Jesus and of the love you have for all the saints.'* (Colossians 1:4)

In fact because we have this kind of hope at work within us it motivates our lives in a God-ward direction and leads to purity of life (1 John 3:3). But when the time of weakness comes because our hope is in the Lord, our souls are anchored and our will is strengthened in the Spirit.

> *'A horse is a vain hope for deliverance; despite all its great strength it cannot save. [18] But the eyes of the LORD are on those who fear him, on those whose hope is in his unfailing love, [19] to deliver them from death and keep them alive in famine. [20] We wait in hope for the LORD; he is our help and our shield. [21] In him our hearts rejoice, for we trust in his holy name. [22] May your unfailing love rest upon us, O LORD, even as we put our hope in you.*
> (Psalm 33:17–22)

People who put their hope in the ability of another person or thing will surely be disappointed at some point but those who put their hope in God will surely be saved. Ungodly hope often leads to wickedness, violence, selfishness or other sin when it is disappointed as is seen in the book of Acts.

Paul and Silas decided to cast a spirit of fortune-telling out of a slave girl who had been pestering them. When the owners realised that their hope of making money was gone, they brought them before the magistrates and made out they were causing trouble.

> 'She kept this up for many days. Finally Paul became so troubled that he turned around and said to the spirit, "In the name of Jesus Christ I command you to come out of her!" At that moment the spirit left her. [19] When the owners of the slave girl realized that their hope of making money was gone, they seized Paul and Silas and dragged them into the marketplace to face the authorities. [20] They brought them before the magistrates and said, "These men are Jews, and are throwing our city into an uproar [21] by advocating customs unlawful for us Romans to accept or practice."' (Acts 16:18–21)

Ungodly hope reacts in this manner because at the core it has selfish ambition at heart, but Godly hope is focused on God.

Conclusion

Once the seat of the will is redirected so that it is no longer seated in the soul or the flesh but in the spirit we can then look at how to enhance aspects of our personality for God. Unfortunately we can not look at every little aspect as this is outside the bounds of this book but we can look at some important ones that will help us on our journey of enhancing our personality for God.

Chapter 5

Developing a Faith-Filled Personality

One important aspect of our personality that needs to alter is how we acquire our perspective on things. *'Perspective affects and shapes our emotions'*. One of the things that highlighted this to me was meeting people who had diametrically opposed levels of faith. I asked one believer how things were. He proceeded to tell me how bad matters were and he suggested that nobody really cared anyway. He reeled off a catalogue of problems and it seemed that the list was endless. After about twenty minutes of listening I tried to persuade him that the Lord was in control and that he need not worry. He listened for a couple of minutes and carried on for another twenty minutes trying to persuade me why it was not that simple. I soon wished that I had never asked. Emotionally my friend was in a mess and no matter how hard I seemed to try I could not get him to raise his perspective and fix his eyes on Jesus. His eyes were fixed on his circumstances and this was affecting his emotions.

(a) Developing the Higher Perspective

In contrast to my friend above, a few months later I arrived at a place in Avon and met a man called Andrew and his wife Grace (we will use Andrew as an example throughout this chapter). They both made an impact upon me from the moment I met them. Andrew led a small group of people who were experiencing an exciting move of God. The minute I met him my faith rose and I began to wonder if revival would not start in this remote corner of England. By the time the meeting started I was so built up in my faith and so excited that I felt ready for anything. From the moment I met that couple till the moment I left, my faith grew and I was left in no doubt that God was going to do wonderful things in that area. A year later I learned that the group along with some other couples were being used to establish a church that has grown from a handful to over one hundred and twenty in one year.

I later thought about Andrew and his wife. His personality exuded confidence in God and he was able to raise my perspective so easily. His ability to see with the eye of faith reminded me of the prophet Elisha. *'The spiritual perspective sees with faith and compassion while a natural perspective sees with doubt and desperation'*. Elisha and his servant were at Dothan where the King of Aram had sent soldiers to capture him. On arrival the soldiers surrounded the city. When Elisha's servant got up the next morning and saw the force attacking them he was terrified. He saw things through the eye of doubt and desperation.

'When the servant of the man of God got up and went out early the next morning, an army with horses and chariots had surrounded the city. **"O, my lord, what shall we do?"** *the servant asked.* [16] *"Don't be afraid," the prophet answered. "Those who are with us are more than those who are with them."* [17] *And Elisha prayed, "O LORD, open his eyes so he may see." Then the LORD opened the servant's eyes, and he looked and saw the hills full of horses and chariots of fire all around Elisha.* [18] *As the enemy came down toward him, Elisha prayed to the LORD, "Strike these people with blindness." So he struck them with blindness, as Elisha had asked.* [19] *Elisha told them, "This is not the road and this is not*

> *the city. Follow me, and I will lead you to the man you are looking for." And he led them to Samaria.* ²⁰ *After they entered the city, Elisha said, "LORD, open the eyes of these men so they can see." Then the LORD opened their eyes and they looked, and there they were, inside Samaria.'*
>
> (2 Kings 6:14–20)

When Elisha prayed he asked God to open his servant's eyes. He had a different viewpoint as he was able to see what was invisible to the naked eye. He saw the spiritual forces of God ready to do God's battle against their enemies if need be. Elisha could not be afraid; his emotions were in a place of security because of his perspective. After his prayer Elisha's servant's perspective also changed from a purely natural one to a spiritual one. Jesus is another example of one who had a spiritual perspective. Even He was affected by what He saw. When He arrived at where His friend Lazarus's family were mourning He began to cry Himself.

> *'Then when Mary was come where Jesus was, and saw him, she fell down at his feet, saying unto him, Lord, if thou hadst been here, my brother had not died.* ³³ *When Jesus therefore saw her weeping, and the Jews also weeping which came with her, he groaned in the spirit, and was troubled,* ³⁴ *And said, Where have ye laid him? They said unto him, Lord, come and see.* ³⁵ *Jesus wept.'*
>
> (John 11:32–35)

Jesus was moved to tears by what He saw just like any man. Yet there was a difference. His tears were tears of compassion not tears of desperation. He knew God was going to raise Lazarus and so He had a higher perspective. Like Jesus, we need a spiritual perspective if our faith is going to enhance our personalities for God, because, when things get difficult **'the spiritual perspective sees with faith and compassion whilst a natural perspective sees with doubt and desperation'**.

(b) Acquiring the Nature of Faith

I have often met people who seemed desperate to work themselves into a place of faith, with the emphasis on emotional work. What they don't realise is that this is the wrong way round. Faith can only grow when we believe the right things, not when we work ourselves into a state of excitement. Having done a scriptural study on the meaning of faith I realise that what Andrew had was a faith-filled personality that embodied the very meaning of the word.

The word *'faith'* can be used to mean *'doctrine or, basically the faith'*, or to speak of the action of putting trust in or upon someone or something. Whatever the use the word has its root in a prime Greek verb *'peitho'*, which means 'to convince or persuade'. Faith in God is basically a persuasion and conviction about the character and integrity of God. This perspective of God is the only setting in which faith can grow.

The Greek word 'faithful' (*'pistis'*) also finds its root from this word which implies the individual is trustworthy, believable, sure, true, and faithful, thus he expresses *'the nature of faith'*. Andrew had faith, he was persuaded by God and so was persuasive when he talked about God. He was convinced by God's word and so was convincing when he spoke of God's word. He was assured by the Holy Spirit that God had spoken about blessing our evening meeting on the day we met and so was assuring. Andrew and his wife displayed an incredible amount of confidence and persuasion in God. It challenged me. Their personality was permeated by an assurance in God that was almost tangible. I have since met other individuals of a similar disposition. Andrew had what can only be described as *'the nature of faith'*. A person can be described by *'nature'* as loving because they have a lot of love to give, as sinful because they sin, as joyful because they express joy or as peaceful because they have peace. In the same way as these, we can describe a man as faithful because he has faith.

A person who expresses the nature of faith or faithfulness,

is expressing a believable, sure and reliable character; the same kind of attributes that God expresses in His relationship with man.

> *'All the ways of the LORD are loving and faithful for those who keep the demands of his covenant.'*
>
> (Psalm 25:10)

The Holy Spirit wants to work such an attitude into our lives (Galatians 5:22). When we eventually arrived at the meeting that evening with Andrew and Grace, God healed, saved and baptised people in the Holy Spirit. Everything Andrew was believing for came to pass. He had a higher perspective.

How can we acquire this *'nature of faith'*? The good news is that our faith can grow till it becomes a manifest aspect of our personality. ***'The nature of faith is tangible and so the nature of faith becomes visible'.***

Weigh up your responses in different situations that affect your walk with the Lord. ***'Your perspective affects how you respond and this response reveals the nature of your faith'.*** Take David when he faced Goliath. He showed how different his perspective was to those around him.

> *'David said to the Philistine, "You come against me with sword and spear and javelin, but I come against you in the name of the LORD Almighty, the God of the armies of Israel, whom you have defied.* [46] *This day the LORD will hand you over to me, and I'll strike you down and cut off your head. Today I will give the carcasses of the Philistine army to the birds of the air and the beasts of the earth, and the whole world will know that there is a God in Israel.* [47] *All those gathered here will know that it is not by sword or spear that the LORD saves; for the battle is the Lord's, and he will give all of you into our hands."'*
>
> (1 Samuel 17:44–47)

David could take Goliath on because he was persuaded

about God's nature. His faith in God's faithfulness and ability to keep His covenant (word), would not be diminished by the size of any obstacle he had to face. He had a bigger perspective of God than the rest of the Israelite army which was terrified at the appearance of Goliath. **'Your perspective will affect your response and also reveals the nature of your faith'**. David's perspective affected his response. As far as he was concerned and regardless of how dark the valley he would fear no evil (Psalm 23:4). He had faith because he meditated on God's word. His faith was tangible and so became visible.

> *'Blessed is the man who does not walk in the counsel of the wicked or stand in the way of sinners or sit in the seat of mockers. *²* But his delight is in the law of the LORD, and on his law he meditates day and night. *³* He is like a tree planted by streams of water, which yields its fruit in season and whose leaf does not wither. Whatever he does prospers.'* (Psalm 1:1–3)

Like David, through meditation on God's word we can acquire and grow in the nature of faith. This is something that we can all do.

(c) Our Personalities are Seeded with Faith

According to Jesus saving faith has come to us in a manner likened to seed sown by a farmer (Luke 8:7–8). Jesus explained that the seed in the parable of the sower is actually the very words of God Himself.

> *'This is the meaning of the parable: The seed is the word of God.'* (Luke 8:11)

God's word is seed that can find place in the life of a man because faith comes by hearing the word of God, and it is because this seed has found place in our lives that we can be saved.

> *'Now that you have purified yourselves by obeying the truth so that you have sincere love for your brothers, love one another deeply, from the heart. ²³ For you have been born again, not of perishable seed, but of imperishable, through the living and enduring word of God.'*
>
> (1 Peter 1:22–23)

And so it is indisputable that *'the born-again believer's personality is seeded with and in faith'*. We have faith because the imperishable word of God is implanted into us. That seed has the power to produce a hundredfold what was sown. The growth of this seed in the life of a believer is what makes a difference to the measure of faith that he has. When the disciples could not heal a little boy Jesus put it down to the amount of faith that they possessed. He did not say that they had no faith He only said that they had little faith (Matthew 17:16–21). As we allow the seed to grow the farmer will eventually produce a crop from it, thirty, sixty or a hundred times what was sown (Luke 8:8). Our faith will eventually grow and become capable of producing the volume of fruit Jesus said it would. The more seed planted the greater the harvest, because *'a farmer can only reap a harvest in proportion to what has been sown into the ground'*. Similarly our personalities can only reap a harvest of good things in proportion to God's word as sown into our lives.

> *'He also said, "This is what the kingdom of God is like. A man scatters seed on the ground. ²⁷ Night and day, whether he sleeps or gets up, the seed sprouts and grows, though he does not know how. ²⁸ All by itself the soil produces grain – first the stalk, then the head, then the full kernel in the head. ²⁹ As soon as the grain is ripe, he puts the sickle to it, because the harvest has come."'*
>
> (Mark 4:26–29)

God wants us to be productive, therefore we must nurture His word which is the seed He has planted in us by meditating on it day and night that we might be successful in

Enhancing Your Personality for God

everything He gives us to do (Psalm 1:1-3). Such people have a perspective that is constantly being shaped by the word of God. But how do we know if our perspectives have been shaped by the seed of God's word, somebody's opinion, fear or even demonic activity? The answer is quite straightforward. If we want to know where our faith is at, or what our perspective is, then, all we have to do is listen to what we say because **'perspective is revealed by what is said and what is said reveals the nature of your faith'**. What we believe in our heart eventually comes out of our mouth and is either in line with God's word or it is not.

> *'But what does it say? "The word is near you; it is in your mouth and in your heart," that is, the word of faith we are proclaiming: ^{9} That if you confess with your mouth, "Jesus is Lord," and believe in your heart that God raised him from the dead, you will be saved.'*
>
> (Romans 10:8-9)

If what we say is not in line with what God says about us then we need to feed ourselves with what He says on an issue, change our attitude and mind on the subject, and get it into line with God's word. Then what we say will change. I am not into positive confession or believing in believing but I am into changing my mind and positively agreeing with what God has said. Elisha's perspective was different to his servants, so what he said was different and how he responded was different. David's perspective was different so what he said when he faced Goliath was uncompromising. Joshua and Caleb had a different report from the other spies when they came back from spying out the land. They had a different perspective and what they believed came out in what they said. The nature of their faith was in keeping with **'the nature of faith'**, which is certain and confident in God.

> *'Then Caleb silenced the people before Moses and said, "We should go up and take possession of the land, for we*

can certainly do it." [31] *But the men who had gone up with him said, "We can't attack those people; they are stronger than we are."* [32] *And they spread among the Israelites a bad report about the land they had explored. They said, "The land we explored devours those living in it. All the people we saw there are of great size.* [33] *We saw the Nephilim there (the descendants of Anak come from the Nephilim). We seemed like grasshoppers in our own eyes, and we looked the same to them."*

(Numbers 13:30–33)

(d) Consistency in Our Personality

If our personalities are to be consistent in the expression of faith then we need faith for day-to-day living. If we want faith for day-to-day living then our fellowship with the Lord must take on greater depth and the highest priority in our life. **'Confidence arises out of being certain of the facts or person you rely on'**. The reason why people have faith for day-to-day living is because they are confident and sure of the person they have believed in and what he has said provides security. It is when we begin to waver in our conviction of Jesus' faithfulness or sway in the trust that He will see us through that we begin to falter. To have faith for day-to-day living Paul says we need to keep our eyes fixed on Christ (Hebrews 12:2–3). Jesus is the author and perfector of our faith, not the pastor or any other human counsellor. Only Jesus can perfect our faith and bring us through into maturity of faith. He, as the author, has a plan written out that will bring us into a place of strength in our faith. Some have fixed their eyes on the church, consequentially they preach the church rather than preach Christ, and so in the time of difficulty often make the mistake of running to the church rather than turn to Christ. Others have fixed their eyes on doctrine or other things that surround Christ and so in the time of difficulty they find themselves lacking in, or, bankrupt in faith, they grow weary and lose heart. They have not fixed their gaze on Christ. Some then blame Him and accuse Him of letting them down, but this is not fair on the Lord because; *'you cannot be convinced by a person unless you have given him time to convince you, you will not trust a person unless you have seen and learned that he is trustworthy'*. Paul's sufferings never dented his convictions; he knew that Jesus was faithful regardless.

'For I am convinced that neither death nor life, neither angels nor demons, neither the present nor the future, nor any powers, ^{39} neither height nor depth, nor anything else in all creation, will be able to separate us from the love of God that is in Christ Jesus our Lord.'
(Romans 8:38–39)

There are different kinds of knowledge. You may know something because you have been told, or you could acquire knowledge because you experience something yourself. The best way to acquire knowledge about a person is not through what you are told about them but by getting to know them yourself. When you take your eyes off Jesus who is the Light of the World how can you see straight? But, when your eyes are fixed on the one who sees and knows everything, He can show you how to get through every hardship. As a result you develop a consistently faithful personality. One scripture that has helped my confidence and faith in the Lord is the account of Him walking on water across a lake.

'Immediately Jesus made his disciples get into the boat and go on ahead of him to Bethsaida, while he dismissed the crowd. ^{46} After leaving them, he went up on a mountainside to pray. ^{47} When evening came, the boat was in the middle of the lake, and he was alone on land. ^{48} He saw the disciples straining at the oars, because the wind was against them. About the fourth watch of the night he went out to them, walking on the lake. He was about to pass by them, ^{49} but when they saw him walking on the lake, they thought he was a ghost. They cried out,

> ^{50} *because they all saw him and were terrified. Immediately he spoke to them and said, "**Take courage! It is I. Don't be afraid.**" ^{51} Then he climbed into the boat with them, and the wind died down. They were completely amazed, ^{52} for they had not understood about the loaves; their hearts were hardened.'* (Mark 6:44–52)

After making his disciples cross the lake Jesus went up the mountain to pray. In the evening He saw the disciples straining when they were about halfway, but notice, He waited until the fourth watch of the night before He went out to meet them. The fourth watch of the night is between three and six in the morning. Jesus saw them struggling during the evening but did not go out to them until the early hours of the morning. He knew what was going on but was not alarmed or troubled. Why did He not rush out to help them immediately? This is the question that most of us ask when in times of difficulty. The reason why Jesus did not rush out was because He had confidence that they would get across because *'He'* had asked them to. After all He is the very word of God himself (John 1:1). As the word of God what He said would come to pass for His word always bears fruit.

> *'As the rain and the snow come down from heaven, and do not return to it without watering the earth and making it bud and flourish, so that it yields seed for the sower and bread for the eater, ^{11} so is my word that goes out from my mouth: It will not return to me empty, but will accomplish what I desire and achieve the purpose for which I sent it. ^{12} You will go out in joy and be led forth in peace; the mountains and hills will burst into song before you, and all the trees of the field will clap their hands.'* (Isaiah 55:10–12)

The astounding thing is that the wind, water and waves did not hinder His progress one iota. He was able to reach them in a very short space of time though they had been struggling all night to get as far as they did. And then when they saw what He did to the waves and the wind they were amazed. The scripture tells us that the reason why they were astonished was because they had hard hearts which they should not have had following the miracles of provision for the multitudes that had occurred just before this boat trip (Mark 6:34-45). Jesus, in feeding the multitude before this boat trip, showed that He was able to provide for people's needs out of the little that they had, even if it was only mustard seed size. Instead of meditation on this in joy they froze in the boat in fear.

Our personalities will strengthen and be more consistent in faith when we realise that just like the incident in the boat Jesus sees exactly where we are at now, but not only this, He sees ahead into the future and everything that happens to us does not take Him by surprise. He knew he was going to be betrayed by Judas (John 13:18-28). He also knew that Peter was going to deny Him three times.

> *'Then Jesus answered, "Will you really lay down your life for me? I tell you the truth, before the rooster crows, you will disown me three times!"'* (John 13:38)

Our circumstances do not take God by surprise. When we realise this it will release us into a new level of faith and trust that God who is faithful will see us through. Acquiring consistency in our personalities arises primarily out of a right perspective and relationship with Jesus which knows that He sees us struggling and will come to save us from difficult circumstances. With this assurance planted in our hearts we can use our faith to see us through. If we are not convinced by God's character then we need to repent of unbelief because it is a sin to consider God as anything but faithful.

After the Holy Spirit illuminated the passage on the lake to me I found that I had a new courage to face trying and difficult circumstances in a way I never had before. My personality has acquired a new confidence in God that I never had before, a resolution to carry on through any difficulty no matter what, because Jesus has convinced me that He is faithful.

(e) The Temperament of Faith

Another interesting revelation that I saw in this account was that in saving his disciples from the storm Jesus manifested *'the temperament of faith'*. In working His miraculous power He took on the attitude of a servant. While I use the term *'nature of faith'* to describe whether the character of a man's faith is constant, sure and certain, I use the term *'the temperament of faith'* to describe the attitude in which this faith is being held.

> *'Your attitude* ('phroneo'), *should be the same as that of Christ Jesus:* [6] *Who, being in very nature God, did not consider equality with God something to be grasped,* [7] *but made himself nothing, taking the very nature of a servant, being made in human likeness.* [8] *And being found in appearance as a man, he humbled himself and became obedient to death – even death on a cross!'*
>
> (Philippians 2:4–8)

The word for attitude used in verse five is the word *'phroneo'*. It means 'to exercise the mind in a given direction', it means 'to set one's affections, mind or thoughts on something'. Hence the King James Version translates verse five as **'Let this mind be in you, which was also in Christ Jesus'**. The Lord requires that in the exercise of our faith we must take on the temperament and attitude of a servant (Mark 9:35). With some individuals the exercise of faith seems to be limited to a narrow desire to see a few good miracles, signs and wonders. In others the exercise of faith seems to come across with a boastful attitude through which Lordship rather than obedience to the Lord is expressed. This should never be our motivation. An individual who has great faith will have the temperament of a servant in the utilization of his faith and consistency in his lifestyle.

> '*When Jesus had entered Capernaum, a centurion came to him, asking for help.* [6] **"Lord,"** *he said, "my servant lies at home paralysed and in terrible suffering."* [7] *Jesus said to him, "I will go and heal him."* [8] *The centurion replied, "****Lord****, I do not deserve to have you come under my roof. But just say the word, and my servant will be healed.* [9] *For I myself am a man under authority, with soldiers under me. I tell this one, 'Go,' and he goes; and that one, 'Come,' and he comes. I say to my servant, 'Do this,' and he does it."* [10] *When Jesus heard this, he was astonished and said to those following him, "I tell you the truth, I have not found anyone in Israel with such great faith."'* (Matthew 8:4–10)

In our relationship with God we are sons, something we ought to proclaim loudly, but nevertheless in our service for and to God we are servants and this should come across as we work for God. Some of the greatest men of God have been the most humble. The Apostle Paul is one such example. Once the *'seed of faith'* is imparted into us we must use the talents that God has given to us in a way that is pleasing to God (Matthew 25:19–21). An individual who has great faith will also have a humility that marks him out as a servant in God's kingdom, but this modesty is not a hindrance to asking God to provide. On the contrary faith will only please God when it expects God to provide and persists until He does.

> '*By faith Enoch was taken from this life, so that he did not experience death; he could not be found, because God had taken him away. For before he was taken, he was commended as one who pleased God.* [6] *And without faith it is impossible to please God, because anyone who comes to him must believe that he exists and that he rewards those who earnestly seek him.*' (Hebrews 11:4–6)

Faith implanted in our personality in seed will grow even faster and be able to overcome when we learn how to persist until we receive from God (Luke 8:1–8). Persistence in asking God is required from us by God and reveals to us whether we actually have a conviction (faith) in God's faithfulness and integrity. The reason why we often do not receive is because we do not persist. Genuine faith will persist until God grants an answer. Genuine faith also receives because it asks with the right motivation.

> *'What causes fights and quarrels among you? Don't they come from your desires that battle within you?* ^{2} *You want something but don't get it. You kill and covet, but you cannot have what you want. You quarrel and fight. You do not have, because you do not ask God.* ^{3} *When you ask, you do not receive, because you ask with wrong motives, that you may spend what you get on your pleasures.* ^{4} ***You adulterous people***, *don't you know that friendship with the world is hatred toward God? Anyone who chooses to be a friend of the world becomes an enemy of God.'* (James 4:1–4)

Adulterous people are basically unfaithful people. We become unfaithful to God when we distrust Him. Adulterers are people who break faith with their partner. We have a relationship with God in which we either remain faithful or break faith. Doubt is a breaking of good faith with God and hampers our personality.

(f) Removing Doubt from Our Personalities

The opposite of faith is doubt **not** unbelief as a lot of people think. Because faith means *'certainty'* the opposite of being certain is to doubt, to have misgivings and to be unsure. Unbelief on the other hand does not believe what is being proposed. As a result doubt must be tackled for what it is – a lack of certainty about God – and not as unbelief, which is slightly different to doubt. If you try and apply the wrong medicine to a sickness then the person will not get better. If you try and deal with doubt but apply remedies applicable to

unbelief the person will not be helped with his problem, because where doubt is simply not yet fully certain, unbelief has made up its mind and hardened itself against God. Doubt has many drawbacks including:
(1) Doubt hinders prayers: (Matthew 21:21).
(2) Doubt condemns us in actions of which we are not sure: (Romans 14:22–23).
(3) Doubt hinders us worshipping God: (Matthew 28:17).
(4) Doubt does not receive from God: (James 1:6–7).
(5) Doubt robs us of our faith for day-to-day living.

Doubt is an intellectual stance that we take towards a situation because we do not know the whole truth. There are different types of doubt but whatever type of doubt we as individuals possess it is always concerned with the question of what is true and what can we be certain of. When it is applied to God then it also includes the question of trust and takes on a serious dimension.

> *'Do not let your hearts be troubled. Trust in God; trust also in me.'*
> (John 14:1)

Types of doubt

'Sceptical doubt' is one type of doubt that we often encounter. I had a friend who was like this. He was always sceptical about people, but professed a faith in God. Whenever he made a comment about a person he was always dismissive about their character motivation, walk with God or some other aspect about that person. He was the epitome of scepticism. The sceptic doubts because he is not sure that you can be certain. Where he is in greatest danger is that he often doubts despite the evidence and continues to question and struggles to be certain about a person's character. Then there is *'persuadable doubt'*. This kind of doubter asks questions because he wants to become certain like Thomas. He knows clearly what will make him certain. He does not ask God for outlandish signs, only for the same experience as his peers because he also wants to believe.

> *'Now Thomas (called Didymus), one of the Twelve, was not with the disciples when Jesus came. [25] So the other disciples told him, "We have seen the Lord!" But he said to them, "Unless I see the nail marks in his hands and put my finger where the nails were, and put my hand into his side, I will not believe it."* (John 20:24–25)

Another kind of doubter is the *'uninformed doubter'*. He doubts because he is unaware but when you try and educate him he is often proud and refuses to accept the truth. One more type is the *'intellectual doubter'*. He finds himself doubting because he cannot work it out and thinks that there must be more to God than the simplistic approach adopted by Christians. There are many other types of doubt.

Elements involved in doubting

Not only is the intellect involved, the emotions are involved in doubting. The problem with doubt is that often in the face of the truth we can carry on doubting simply because it makes us feel comfortable. Believing the truth carries implications, commitments and changes in our lifestyles. Such pressure could at times cause us to choose to doubt even though we know the truth. There is no shortcut to getting rid of doubt. Whatever the type, repentance and a commitment to hold on to the seed of God's word is required (John 8:31–37).

Conclusion

Our personalities will become not only consistent when we put these principles into practice, the seed God has planted in us will cause us to produce much fruit and express the nature, temperament and perspective of faith in our personality.

Chapter 6

Developing a Joy and Praise-Filled Personality

(a) Positive Attributes are Acquirable

Many people have noticed others whom they regard as having a pleasant personality and desire the same themselves. It is possible to acquire exciting attributes and other aspects to our personality. Now that we know the glorious wonder of how to reseat our will in the spirit and to anchor our emotions, we can jettison those things in our soulish realm that hinder and bind, and acquire emotions that enhance our personality for God. There are many expressions of the soul. We could enhance our expression of love, patience, kindness, gentleness or other things but in this chapter we will only concentrate on two, *'Joy'* and *'Praise'* and from them pick up certain keys that will help in acquiring and expressing godly attributes. Joy and praise will set the backdrop to understanding how in every realm we can learn to become obedient to other qualities and traits God would have us develop. If you are going to express praise it must be in the way God wants you to; if you are going to express love it must also be in the way God wants you to.

In our example of joy certain features come out. Isaiah is often a man who comes out as being serious but in Isaiah chapter 61 he exhibits an expression of joy that perhaps does not fit into our stereotyped image of him.

> *'I delight greatly in the* LORD; *my soul rejoices in my God. For he has clothed me with garments of salvation and arrayed me in a robe of righteousness, as a bridegroom adorns his head like a priest, and as a bride adorns herself with her jewels.'* (Isaiah 61:10)

The Hebrew word used here is quite revealing. It is the word *'giyl'* which means 'to spin around under the influence of a strong emotion'. What produced this strong expression of emotion? In verses one to nine he tells us that he had just received a revelation of the anointing of the Spirit that was coming upon Christ (Isaiah 61:1–4; *cf.* Luke 4:18). When he realised that captives would be liberated, those who mourned would be comforted, provision would be made for those who grieved, bestowing crowns of beauty and the oil of gladness, Isaiah became ecstatic. He said his soul caused him to rejoice or spin around under the influence of this revelation. I tried to picture Isaiah doing a twirl and found it amusing, but this is exactly what he did. ***'Joyful emotions are developed from meditating on the works of God'***. This provides us with the first key for acquiring godly attributes:

Key 1: *'Godly emotions arise out of the revelation that comes from meditating on the acts of God'*.

Isaiah rejoiced because he had thought through the implications of the anointing of the Holy Spirit on Jesus. There is always a manifestation when we are filled with a godly emotion like joy, ranging from a smile to spinning around emotionally like Isaiah. Jesus encouraged such external manifestation.

> *'Blessed are you when people insult you, persecute you and falsely say all kinds of evil against you because of me.* [12] *Rejoice* (aggallio) *and be glad, because great is*

your reward in heaven, for in the same way they persecuted the prophets who were before you.'

(Matthew 5:11–12)

He explains here that our response to persecution should be to *'leap for joy'*, which is what *'aggallio'* means. He encouraged His disciples to meditate on the reward that awaits them in heaven not on the pain and difficulty they would go through. Luke remembers Jesus say more than just leap for joy. He recalls Jesus telling His disciples to *'skip for joy'* as well which is what *'skirtao'* means.

'Looking at his disciples, he said: "Blessed are you who are poor, for yours is the kingdom of God. [21] Blessed are you who hunger now, for you will be satisfied. Blessed are you who weep now, for you will laugh. [22] Blessed are you when men hate you, when they exclude you and insult you and reject your name as evil, because of the Son of Man. [23] Rejoice (skirtao) *in that day and leap for joy* (aggallio), *because great is your reward in heaven. For that is how their fathers treated the prophets."'*

(Luke 6:20–23)

The first time I ever saw this happen was on an American air force base where the pastor skipped around the hall during the time of praise and worship. It was a most extraordinary sight as this pastor rejoiced mightily before the Lord. In comparison I felt-flat footed and awkward. I realised that his expression of joy was in no way hindered by his self-consciousness; what he felt in his heart he could physically express. In this respect he was like a child who whooped and danced for joy because of what he felt about God. This is the gateway to the second key towards acquiring godly attributes in our personality:

Key 2: *'Expression should be the natural choice following godly emotions'.*

Just like a child naturally dances on the spot when given a present or sweet, the physical manifestation of pleasure is the natural response when rejoicing in God. Embarrassment or self-consciousness can be a hinderance but overcoming this is best taken one step at a time. If you feel joy lift up your hands and simply allow what you feel to be expressed. If you can not yet lift your hands in a meeting then tap your feet, but whatever you do, choose to manifest what you feel. Some Christians unfortunately try and do it the other way round. They work themselves into an emotional state through music or other means, they have a great time but later wonder why they felt so good and don't understand why they have not changed much given the wonderful feelings they had. Instead of the feelings coming out of a revelation of God's works or word they came out of music or other things that can make one feel good. Only a revelation of God and His abilities will enable us to change adequately. Once the revelation comes we should allow ourselves to physically manifest and *'express'* godly feelings that arise out of meditating on God.

To put the first two keys into operation might be helpful at this point. Suppose I wanted to express a greater degree of love because I felt that I was lacking in this area, this is what I would do. Firstly, I would meditate on the love of God, thus implementing the first key. Then because of what His word causes me to realise and see, I hopefully would choose to respond to the conviction of God's word, which is utilising the second key. I would hopefully act out of conviction from His word and express it in a greater degree of love. This is how I seek to deal with issues in my life. If while I am meditating on God's word I realise that I need to repent then I repent. The feelings provided by His word at work within me make it easier to choose to change, so if I am being impatient, reading from the scriptures how God exercises patience towards me produces a conviction which causes me to apply more patience myself. We need the convicting power of God's word and Spirit to change.

God taught His people to *'express'* the feelings which have arisen within them due to the work of His word at work inside them. When He led them into the promised land He taught them to express their joy in giving a loud shout (Joshua 6:1–5), and when they did, God used their shout to bring down the walls of Jericho, opening it up for them to attack. Expressing godly feelings is an important command in Scripture.

> *'Clap your hands, all you nations; shout to God with cries of joy.'* (Psalm 47:1)

I have often been amused to at how culture seems to help one group of people become known for particular traits. I have noticed in some meetings that black people in Africa seem to be more extrovert and outgoing whilst white people in Britain appear to be more reserved. Though we should not over-generalise, the reason why one group of people have particular traits is because they have trained themselves to behave in that manner. And so in Pentecostal churches the members have trained themselves to physically and verbally manifest during the preaching of the word. Like the people of Jericho they verbally express their exhilaration at the wonder of God; whilst though they may feel the same exhilaration, the believers in some Baptist churches generally listen in silence.

(b) Praise-Filled People Boast

To develop a joy and praise-filled personality for God we cannot evade this expressive aspect. Vocalising our praise for God expresses our deep satisfaction in God's actions.

> *'You who fear the LORD, praise* ('halal') *him! All you descendants of Jacob, honour him! Revere him, all you descendants of Israel!'* (Psalm 22:23)

The kind of praise spoken of here is **'halal'**. It is from this Hebrew word that we get the word **'hallelujah'**. **'Halal'** means 'to boast about, to make shine, to make clear'. When it is applied to the Lord in the term *'hallelujah'* it means 'to boast about the Lord', 'to cause the Lord to shine' or 'to make the Lord clear'. This is the third key to developing a godly expression of the soul:

Key 3: *'The confession of our revelation requires us to take a godly position in situations'*.

This is very important because until we speak out what we know or believe of God without reservation then we are taking a position of non-commitment. Personalities that express joy and praise have taken a stance of commitment with respect to God. *'Halal'* towards God is boasting about God. Praise in this form should be a natural outworking of our relationship with God because He has placed on us a garment of praise. If we wrongly identify this boasting in praise as being extrovert then it may well cause us to refrain from boasting. Boasting in God is natural, regardless of temperament.

> *'and provide for those who grieve in Zion – to bestow on them a crown of beauty instead of ashes, the oil of gladness instead of mourning, and a garment of praise* ('halal') *instead of a spirit of despair. They will be called oaks of righteousness, a planting of the* LORD *for the display of his splendour.* (Isaiah 61:3)

Our personalities are clothed with boasting of God. If we do not boast about God it is like putting a good suit in a wardrobe. Believers can, in all their actions, boast about God regardless of circumstances, whoever they are and whatever our circumstances. This is the fourth key:

Key 4: *'Boastful praise is one of the external spiritual garments of all believers'*.

But it is easy to develop a personality that is praise-filled or joyful without that joy or praise being derived from God. Sarah's beauty is one such example. When Abraham went to Egypt the Egyptian officials saw that she was very beautiful:

> *'When Abram came to Egypt, the Egyptians saw that she was a very beautiful woman. [15] And when Pharaoh's officials saw her, they praised ('halal') her to Pharaoh, and she was taken into his palace.'* (Genesis 12:14–15)

They praised (*'halal'*) or boasted about her to Pharaoh. Here we see that it is possible to attract praise because of some aspect of our personality but not necessarily have God at the centre of the praise that is being expressed. To enhance our personality for God we need to be clear about who it is we are actually boasting about, because praise, if it is not of God, can verge on idolatry which brings the wrath of God, as was brought down on the Philistines after they had captured Samson. They proceeded to make sport of him and boasted (*'halal'*) about their god Dagon, saying he was the one who had given Samson into their hands.

It was this, coupled with Samson's repentance, that caused God to give him back his strength so that he could overcome his enemies (Judges 16:23–31). Praise-filled personalities that are enhanced for God attract praise themselves, not because of their own ability but as a direct consequence of God's involvement in that person's life. They are praised primarily because they stand out for God and themselves boast about God. Job was one such individual. His fame stretched to the very heavens (Job 1:8). He was known as a righteous and upright man and even when he lost all of his family he refused to say one bad word against God (Job 2:9–10). Nevertheless he looked back and longed for the time when God blessed him.

> *'Oh, for the days when I was in my prime, when God's intimate friendship blessed my house, [5] when the Almighty was still with me and my children were around me, [6] when my path was drenched with cream and the*

> *rock poured out for me streams of olive oil. ⁷ When I went to the gate of the city and took my seat in the public square, ⁸ the young men saw me and stepped aside and the old men rose to their feet; ⁹ the chief men refrained from speaking and covered their mouths with their hands; ¹⁰ the voices of the nobles were hushed, and their tongues stuck to the roof of their mouths. ¹¹ Whoever heard me spoke well of me, and those who saw me commended me, ¹² because I rescued the poor who cried for help, and the fatherless who had none to assist him. ¹³ The man who was dying blessed me; I made the widow's heart sing.'* (Job 29:4–13)

How he described this period in his life is quite extraordinary. It was a time when God so blessed him that no matter how hard the ground was it would produce for him in a manner likened to rocks pouring forth precious oil. The reason he gives for living in this wonderful state is in the first verses.

> *'Job continued his discourse: ² "How I long for the months gone by, for the days when God watched over me, ³ when his lamp shone* ('halal') *upon my head and by his light I walked through darkness!"'* (Job 29:1–3)

He attributed his state of blessedness to the fact that God boasted (*'halal'*) about him. God is the one who *'shone'* (*'halal'*) upon him and made him great. This brings us to the fifth key:

Key 5: *'Praising God attracts praise from God'*.

Job regarded the fruit of God praising him as enabling him to walk through any darkness. This is not surprising. If he who said let there be light chooses to speak well of us how can His words fail to produce great fruit in our lives? Job praised God in how he lived and so God boasted about Job.

God caused Job to shine. One can receive praise from a man and feel good as a result of it, but the praise that comes from God does us so much more good. But in order to receive praise from God like Job, we must not allow anything else to receive our *'halal'* or boasting that is due to God, no matter how attractive those other things appear.

> *'if I have regarded the sun in its radiance* ('halal') *or the moon moving in splendour,* [27] *so that my heart was secretly enticed and my hand offered them a kiss of homage,* [28] *then these also would be sins to be judged, for I would have been unfaithful to God on high.'*
> (Job 31:26–28)

The praise-filled personality will attract praise from God and as a result fare well, because when God speaks well of us like Job, we surely must find the resources to walk through any darkness. Not only does God praise such a person, others will find their works worthy of praise because of their relationship with God.

> *'Charm is deceptive, and beauty is fleeting; but a woman who fears the LORD is to be praised* ('halal'). [31] *Give her the reward she has earned, and let her works bring her praise* ('halal') *at the city gate.'* (Proverbs 31:30–31)

(c) The Praise-Filled Personality Confesses to God

Praise is not just verbal acknowledgment of God. In the Old Testament we learn the individual who offers up praise to God gives themselves in their praise of God.

> *'She conceived again, and when she gave birth to a son she said, "This time I will praise* ('yadah') *the LORD." So she named him Judah. Then she stopped having children.'*
> (Genesis 29:35)

The word praise used here is the word *'yadah'* which comes from the word *'hand'*. 'Yadah' is praise that is rendered with outstretched hands. It means *'to confess, to praise, to give thanks'*. When this type of praise is offered up in the atmosphere of repentance it is considered to be confession.

> *'Or if a person thoughtlessly takes an oath to do anything, whether good or evil – in any matter one might carelessly swear about – even though he is unaware of it, in any case when he learns of it he will be guilty. ^{5} When anyone is guilty in any of these ways, he must confess* ('yadah') *in what way he has sinned.'* (Leviticus 5:4–5)

The praise-filled personality comes to God with hands open and filled with something to give to God, but where he finds sin he openly confesses, which is giving praise to God. This is what Aaron was commanded to do when making atonement for Israel's sin.

> *'When Aaron has finished making atonement for the Most Holy Place, the Tent of Meeting and the altar, he shall bring forward the live goat. ^{21} He is to lay both hands on the head of the live goat and confess* ('Yadah') *over it all the wickedness and rebellion of the Israelites – all their sins – and put them on the goat's head. He shall send the goat away into the desert in the care of a man appointed for the task.'* (Leviticus 16:20–21)

Often people find it difficult to praise God in worship because they have not praised God in repentance:

Key 6: *'To praise God in worship you must first praise Him in repentance'*.

To be able to enjoy God's presence and praise Him in sincerity then we must keep short accounts with God. Our personalities are better served when sin is readily admitted and repented of in an attitude that glorifies God and gives thanks to Him for His mercy.

> 'Shouts of joy and victory resound in the tents of the righteous: "The Lord's right hand has done mighty things! [16] The Lord's right hand is lifted high; the Lord's right hand has done mighty things!" [17] I will not die but live, and will proclaim what the LORD has done. [18] The LORD has chastened me severely, but he has not given me over to death. [19] Open for me the gates of righteousness; I will enter and give thanks ('yadah') to the LORD. [20] This is the gate of the LORD through which the righteous may enter. [21] I will give you thanks, for you answered me; you have become my salvation.'
> (Psalm 118:14–21)

(d) The Praise-Filled Personality Sings Praise to God

Joan came into the church bubbling over in song; she was humming to herself as she arranged the flowers. All the humming was done without any hint of being self-conscious. Praise-filled personalities enjoy praising God in song and are often so infectious with the freedom they enjoy that it helps others enter into that realm of praise.

> 'Hear, O LORD, and have mercy upon me: LORD, be thou my helper. [11] Thou hast turned for me my mourning into dancing: thou hast put off my sackcloth, and girded me with gladness; [12] To the end that my glory may sing ('zamar') praise to thee, and not be silent. O LORD my God, I will give thanks unto thee for ever.'
> (Psalm 30:10–12 KJV)

Singing is therapeutic and so many people love singing. When it is offered up to God in praise there is a supernatural benefit that comes with it. Some of this benefit is revealed in the Psalms.

> *'Their fruit shalt thou destroy from the earth, and their seed from among the children of men. [11] For they intended evil against thee: they imagined a mischievous device, which they are not able to perform. [12] Therefore shalt thou make them turn their back, when thou shalt make ready thine arrows upon thy strings against the face of them. [13] Be thou exalted, Lord, in thine own strength: so will we sing ('zamar') and praise thy power.'*
> (Psalm 21:10–13 KJV)

The psalmist here is considering the fate of wicked men. In his deliberations he says he will *'zamar'* which means *'to sing praises'*. It is particularly used of praise accompanied by stringed instruments. In the revelation that the psalmist has he knows that God will play *'strings'* as well. He will pluck the strings of a bow and fire arrows. He will make them turn their back by *'Playing stings of warfare'* (Psalm 21:12). An interesting thought here is how could God possibly miss? The response of the psalmist is to sing praise to God with stringed instruments. God is playing His strings of warfare against the wicked and so the psalmist played his strings of praise in honour of God.

When people sing praises to God it does more than just make us feel good because God will strengthen such personalities by supernaturally responding to the circumstances. This supernatural strengthening of the personality in praise is further seen in the New Testament.

> *'They brought them before the magistrates and said, "These men are Jews, and are throwing our city into an uproar [21] by advocating customs unlawful for us Romans to accept or practice." [22] The crowd joined in the attack against Paul and Silas, and the magistrates ordered them to be stripped and beaten. [23] After they had been severely flogged, they were thrown into prison, and the jailer was commanded to guard them carefully. [24] Upon receiving such orders, he put them in cells and fastened their feet in the stocks. [25] About midnight Paul and Silas were*

> *praying and singing hymns ('hymneo') to God, and the other prisoners were listening to them.* [26] *Suddenly there was such a violent earthquake that the foundations of the prison were shaken. At once all the prison doors flew open, and everybody's chains came loose.'*
>
> (Acts 16:20-26)

Here the word used is *'hymneo'* which means *'to sing praises'*. Again we see God responding to the praises in song by breaking open the prison doors. In the middle of a difficult time God chose to encourage and affirm His disciples. Singing in the Spirit is the highest form of singing praise to God. Often people find great benefit from singing in the Spirit.

> *'So what shall I do? I will pray with my spirit, but I will also pray with my mind; "**I will sing with my spirit, but I will also sing with my mind**".* [16] *If you are praising God with your spirit, how can one who finds himself among those who do not understand say 'Amen' to your thanksgiving, since he does not know what you are saying?* [17] *You may be giving thanks well enough, but the other man is not edified.* [18] *I thank God that I speak in tongues more than all of you.'* (1 Corinthians 14:14-18)

(e) The Praise-Filled Personality Magnifies God

Nothing appears so beautiful as the image of a godly man or woman. Godly people, by virtue of their godliness, magnify God. In the presence of godly people the sense of awe experienced motivates a desire to emulate such a lifestyle.

The Principal of the Bible College I attended was such a man. He carried with him a peace that was tangible and the respect he commanded was universal. When he taught the scriptures his knowledge of the word fed the heart and filled the mind with wonder. At the end of his class nothing was left but admiration of the man and praise for God. The praise-filled personality attracts praise to God, not just because they can vocalise or express this praise, but because they have proved God's faithfulness to them and similarly show a life of faithfulness to God. The Principal was a gentle man who could in no way be described as extrovert, but every word he uttered about God was in praise, boast or instruction about the Lord. When he spoke about the Lord praise for God poured from his lips. I am sure that we all know individuals who are very expressive in their praise but the point of developing a praise-filled personality is not necessarily to develop a specific type of personality, but to understand what the scripture says praise is and then to begin to do it as an act of obedience to God until it becomes a part of our personality. This is the final key:

Key 7: *'Habitual obedience and performance of any godly attribute turns that attribute into a part of our personality'.*

(f) Reasons Why People Do Not Praise

At one of our conferences I heard Dr Judson Cornwall make this statement:

> 'Even after the facts of praise are well-known, the act of praise is painfully difficult.'

I thought about this and made a mental note. I have covered some of the reasons why people find it hard to praise, like guilt and sin. The biggest problem though is the self. Individuals often find it difficult to give praise to God because they are caught up with a negative or positive perspective of themselves which clouds out God. When there is a negative reason why people chose not to praise, the root of the problem is often fear. In the realm of praise, it is often the fear of ridicule or rejection that makes the expression of praise difficult. When it is an inflated self-consciousness the problem is pride. When we are overly concerned with ourselves we cannot praise God. Events in our lives can be allowed to acquire such a prominent place that they overshadow the Lord, but they must not be allowed to, and since we have been given a garment of praise (*'halal'* or *'boasting'*) instead of a spirit of despair we can make sure they do not (Isaiah 61:3). Other individuals who have been involved in satanic worship or cultic activities usually find it difficult to comfortably enter into praise. Such individuals often need specialised counselling.

Chapter 7

Acquired Characteristics

When we became Christians we acquired and developed new aspects to our personalities that perhaps we do not fully understand. I want to pick out some of these. It would be impossible to express what we have become within the confines of one chapter, but what I will highlight in sections are aspects of our personalities that have changed. We need to begin to understand some of these aspects as this will help us better understand why we behave the way we do and what to expect.

We Have Blessed Personalities

In Matthew chapter five Jesus taught his disciples that they were *'blessed'*. Why do people teach? The motivation behind teaching is so that a way of thinking may be imparted to the hearer. People who teach impart knowledge to the pupil. In Matthew chapter five Jesus was trying to realise the expectations of His disciples by teaching them that they were blessed.

> *'Blessed* ('makarios') *are the poor in spirit, for theirs is the kingdom of heaven.* [4] *Blessed are those who mourn, for they will be comforted.* [5] *Blessed are the meek, for they will inherit the earth.* [6] *Blessed are those who hunger and thirst for righteousness, for they will be*

filled. ⁷ *Blessed are the merciful, for they will be shown mercy.* ⁸ *Blessed are the pure in heart, for they will see God.* ⁹ *Blessed are the peacemakers, for they will be called sons of God.* ¹⁰ *Blessed are those who are persecuted because of righteousness, for theirs is the kingdom of heaven.* ¹¹ *Blessed are you when people insult you, persecute you and falsely say all kinds of evil against you because of me.* ¹² *Rejoice and be glad, because great is your reward in heaven, for in the same way they persecuted the prophets who were before you.'*

(Matthew 5:3–12)

Using the Greek word **'makarios'** which means **'supremely blessed'**, Jesus was explaining to them that even when they were poor in spirit they were **'supremely blessed to the highest degree possible above which there is no greater blessing'**. God is the *'supreme being'* and there is no god supreme to Him. To be supremely blessed means to be blessed of the highest possible order. This is the state even of those who are poor in spirit, because theirs is the kingdom of Heaven. A crushed spirit can cause all kinds of heartache for the individual but when we remember that 'the Kingdom of heaven' is ours it lifts our spirits. Supremely blessed of the highest degree are those who mourn. Why? Because they will be comforted. God will draw them near, as the Counsellor draws close. Supremely blessed of the highest degree above which there is no greater blessing and thus beyond the further possibility of being blessed are those who hunger and thirst for righteousness, for they will be filled. God will provide an abundance, a surplus will be their lot. As the good sheep follow the good Shepherd, He will lead them into an abundance upon which they can gorge. Jesus culminated this teaching by saying supremely blessed are those who are persecuted because of righteousness.

(a) Blessedness has become an attribute

The incredible thing about this *'blessedness'* that Jesus speaks about is that for the believer it is more than just a one-off blessing imparted in a time of crisis. It has become an attribute. Just as God is known as kind, loving and caring, people can by attribute be described as loving or caring, gentle or kind, so *'blessedness'* has acquired the status of an attribute in a believer's life.

> *'What does the Scripture say?* ***"Abraham believed God, and it was credited to him as righteousness."*** [4] *Now when a man works, his wages are not credited to him as a gift, but as an obligation.* [5] *However, to the man who does not work but trusts God who justifies the wicked, his faith is credited as righteousness.* [6] *David says the same thing when he speaks of the* ***blessedness*** *(*'makarismos' – **attribute of good fortune**) *of the man to whom God credits righteousness apart from works:* [7] ***"Blessed*** *(*'makarios' – **supremely blessed**) *are they whose transgressions are forgiven, whose sins are covered."'* (Romans 4:3–8)

The Greek word for *'blessedness'* here is the word *'makarismos'*, which means *'attribute of good fortune, or characteristic of blessedness'*. Paul is saying that believers are in a state of blessedness which has been accredited to them because of their faith in God. Just as a man who works is credited with wages, the man who trusts God is credited as righteous. Such a man is supremely blessed by attribute. People who are subjects of God's kingdom are supremely blessed. Just as kind, caring, gentle and loving people are recognised by attribute, believers ought to be recognised as being blessed by attribute. There ought to be a stream of blessing after blessing accompanying believers.

I can hear the scores of questions which follow such a teaching. They are usually of a very personal and heart rending nature, pointing to some individual, and saying if we are blessed why then is so and so suffering in such a manner? This kind of approach goes from experience and tries to modify the word of God to suit our experience. Unfortunately we learn nothing by this approach but how to justify our experiences. If Jesus said we are supremely blessed then there ought to be tangible evidence of this state of blessing in our lives. This still leaves the question though, why some believers can claim to experience this state of blessedness and others appear not to. I believe that **'If you live in a place long enough you will develop characteristics that mark you out as coming from that place'**. People who live in a place develop an accent which others can distinguish and pick out. I am often amazed that people can at times still pick out elements of a Scottish accent although I spent my teens in Nigeria. An individual who lives in a place will also dress like the locals, acquire a similar taste in food and even be influenced in the way he or she thinks. **'When you live in slavery long enough you develop characteristics that mark you out as a slave'**. Why? Because when you live in a place long enough you develop characteristics that mark you out as coming from that place. The way a slave speaks is different to the way a master speaks, and so you could say his accent is different. The clothes he wears are not quite the best, and the food he eats is usually second rate.

The people of God lived in slavery long enough; they cried out and one day the Lord had mercy and delivered them, sending a man called Moses to take them out of bondage. **'The prodigal son lived the life of a pig and so developed characteristics that marked him out as a pig'**. Why? Because if you live in a place long enough you will develop characteristics that mark you out as coming from that place. He had loose living and so would have had loose speech. He ended up eating the same food as pigs and his clothes smelled as a result. When you live like a pig you develop characteristics that mark you out as being like a pig. **'When you live in the Kingdom of God long enough you develop characteristics that mark you out as coming from that kingdom'**. People who meet believers ought to see something different about them; there ought to be characteristics that mark them out as coming from God's kingdom. Our speech ought to be different. When they begin to speak people recognise that they are not of this world. They have learned how to praise God with their lips, and when they run out of words they burst into songs of praise. They wear clothes that no fashion on earth can match and no tailor could copy. They are clothed in garments of praise and arrayed in a robe of righteousness. Their taste in food is exquisite. As they eat of the best in the land, they can say *'taste and see that the Lord is good'* (Psalm 34:8). They know that He has prepared a table before them in the presence of all their enemies. They consider their cup to be full and running over as God has rescued them and brought them into His Kingdom, a land flowing over with milk and honey. When anybody sees such an individual, just as they recognise an individual who comes from India when they look at him, or a Scotsman when they hear him speak, or a solider from a particular army because of what he wears, they should recognise a believer. Why? Because when you live in the Kingdom of God long enough you develop characteristics that mark you out as coming from that kingdom. Have you been living in the Kingdom long? Then consider what Jesus said. Trust Him and expect that your personality will manifest this attribute of blessedness according to His word.

> *You will be blessed in the city and blessed in the country.*
> *[4] The fruit of your womb will be blessed, and the crops of your land and the young of your livestock – the calves of your herds and the lambs of your flocks. [5] Your basket and your kneading trough will be blessed. [6] You will be blessed when you come in and blessed when you go out. [7] The LORD will grant that the enemies who rise up against you will be defeated before you. They will come at you from one direction but flee from you in seven. [8] The LORD will send a blessing on your barns and on everything you put your hand to. The LORD your God will bless you in the land he is giving you.*
> (Deuteronomy 28:3–8)

(b) You remain blessed because...

Obedience to God is paramount to maintaining a state of blessedness, and although we do not acquire this blessedness through works but by faith in the Lord, disobedience to His word does not solicit God's blessing.

> '*As Jesus was saying these things, a woman in the crowd called out,* **"Blessed is the mother who gave you birth and nursed you."** [28] *He replied,* **"Blessed rather are those who hear the word of God and obey it."**'
>
> (Luke 11:27-28)

Others do not enjoy this state of blessedness because they give up on God halfway through difficulties. **'You enter deception if you think you will be blessed without continuing in obedience'.**

> 'Do not merely listen to the word, and so deceive yourselves. Do what it says. [23] Anyone who listens to the word but does not do what it says is like a man who looks at his face in a mirror [24] and, after looking at himself, goes away and immediately forgets what he looks like. [25] But the man who looks intently into the perfect law that gives freedom, and continues to do this, not forgetting what he has heard, but doing it – he will be blessed ('makarios') in what he does.'
>
> (James 1:22-25)

The attitude we should have ought to be the same as that of Jacob who refused to let God go until He blessed him.

> 'So Jacob was left alone, and a man wrestled with him till daybreak. [25] When the man saw that he could not overpower him, he touched the socket of Jacob's hip so that his hip was wrenched as he wrestled with the man. [26] Then the man said, "Let me go, for it is daybreak." But Jacob replied, "I will not let you go unless you bless me." [27] The man asked him, "What is your name?" "Jacob," he answered. [28] Then the man said, "Your name will no longer be Jacob, but Israel, because you have struggled with God and with men and have overcome."'
>
> (Genesis 32:24-28)

Acquired Characteristics

'Jacob' means *'deceiver'* and this is what he was. He cheated his brother Esau out of his inheritance. God met him and wrestled with him until daybreak. When God saw that He was not going to overpower him He wrenched his hip from his socket but still Jacob refused to let Him go until He blessed him. After God had knocked all the deception out of him He gave him a new name *'Israel'*. Israel means *'struggled with God'*.

> *'God said to him, "Your name is Jacob, but you will no longer be called Jacob; your name will be Israel." So he named him Israel.'* (Genesis 35:10)

This attitude of holding on and not letting go needs to be cultivated if we are to remain in a state of blessing. We have a new name, we are called Christians (1 Peter 4:16), and all our past sins are forgiven. But, if when persecution or difficulty comes along, we let go of God or blame Him, the question is, where is our faith or trust in God? Some backslide so badly after difficulties that it sometimes takes years for them to be restored. Jesus encourages His disciples to adopt this persistent attitude in times of difficulty.

> *'Then Jesus told his disciples a parable to show them that they should always pray and not give up. ² He said: "In a certain town there was a judge who neither feared God nor cared about men. ³ And there was a widow in that town who kept coming to him with the plea, 'Grant me justice against my adversary.' ⁴ For some time he refused. But finally he said to himself, 'Even though I don't fear God or care about men, ⁵ yet because this widow keeps bothering me, I will see that she gets justice, so that she won't eventually wear me out with her coming!'" ⁶ And the Lord said, "Listen to what the unjust judge says. ⁷ And will not God bring about justice for his chosen ones, who cry out to him day and night? Will he keep putting them off?"'* (Luke 18:1–7)

(c) Blessed people are ('eulogeo') blessed

Paul indicates that believers are blessed by and through the Spirit.

> *'Praise be* ('eulogetos') *to the God and Father of our Lord Jesus Christ, who has blessed* ('eulogeo') *us in the heavenly realms with every spiritual blessing* ('eulogia') *in Christ.'*
> (Ephesians 1:3)

As can be seen the word he used is **'*eulogeo*'** which means **'*well spoken of or blessed*'**. It is from this word that we get the English word **'*eulogy*'**, which is speech or writing in praise of a person. Paul is saying that God has spoken well of us in the heavenly realms by means of the Spirit with every spiritual blessing. This God, who through speech brings things to pass, has spoken well of us, and so we will benefit through His irresistible word taking root in our lives. We could translate this passage in Ephesians like this:

> 'Spoken well about and thus Praise is rendered to the God and Father of our Lord Jesus Christ, who has spoken well of us and poured out a benediction upon us in the heavenly realms by means of every spiritual fine and eloquent speaking and commendation about us in Christ...'
> (Ephesians 1:3 Yinka paraphrase)

The result is we **'*eulogetos*'** God, that is we speak well of God. You can not help but speak well of someone who speaks well of you. Unfortunately some people settle for **'*the blessing of the soul*'** which, though powerful, is not as powerful as **'*the blessing of the Spirit*'**. We see the power of the soul when Isaac wanted to exercise the blessing of the soul over his son Esau.

> *'And make me savory meat, such as I love, and bring it to me, that I may eat; that my soul may bless thee before I die.'*
> (Genesis 27:4 KJV)

Rebekah helped her son Jacob deceive Isaac and steal *'the blessing of the soul'* which his father wanted to give to Esau.

> *'And Jacob said unto his father, I am Esau thy firstborn; I have done according as thou badest me: arise, I pray thee, sit and eat of my venison, that thy soul may bless me.'* (Genesis 27:19 KJV)

Later when Esau and Isaac discovered that there had been deception, Isaac said it was too late, Jacob had been blessed and this could not be revoked. He would remain blessed.

> *'Isaac trembled violently and said, "Who was it, then, that hunted game and brought it to me? I ate it just before you came and I blessed him – and indeed he will be blessed!"* [34] *When Esau heard his father's words, he burst out with a loud and bitter cry and said to his father, "Bless me – me too, my father!"'*
> (Genesis 27:33–34)

Although soulish or emotional blessings are powerful, as can be seen from the example above, they are not as powerful as the blessing of the Spirit. In some cases the blessing of the soul is unfortunately wrongly taken as prophecy, which can govern an individual's life. This can happen where an emotional and good desire for blessing is conveyed or taken as prophecy. We all need to be comforted but we should realise that it is the blessing of the Spirit that is the higher principle. The soul took us into bondage; the Spirit brings us into liberty because, where the law of the Spirit is there is liberty. At the end of the day the only reason Isaac's blessing carried any weight was because he himself was blessed of God.

A people who are blessed of God cannot be easily cursed. Consider Balak and Balaam. Balak the King of Moab saw the advancing people of God and wanted them cursed so he asked Balaam to curse them so they would not succeed. But he found that he could not because God had blessed them

(Numbers 22:5, 20–23; 24:12–19). When God has spoken well over us that settles it. He told Moses that He would bring His people out and He did. He told Saul He would take his crown from him and He did. People who are in Christ are spoken well of as they are Abraham's descendants.

> 'Consider Abraham: "He believed God, and it was credited to him as righteousness." [7] Understand, then, that those who believe are children of Abraham. [8] The Scripture foresaw that God would justify the Gentiles by faith, and announced the gospel in advance to Abraham: "All nations will be blessed through you."'
>
> (Galatians 3:6–8)

Those who have faith are blessed along with Abraham. Again we are reminded that this blessing is not one of works.

> 'All who rely on observing the law are under a curse, for it is written: "Cursed is everyone who does not continue to do everything written in the Book of the Law." [11] Clearly no one is justified before God by the law, because, "The righteous will live by faith." [12] The law is not based on faith; on the contrary, "The man who does these things will live by them." [13] Christ redeemed us from the curse of the law by becoming a curse for us, for it is written: "Cursed is everyone who is hung on a tree." [14] He redeemed us in order that the blessing ('eulogia') given to Abraham might come to the Gentiles through Christ Jesus, so that by faith we might receive the promise of the Spirit.'
>
> (Galatians 3:10–14)

God spoke well of Abraham and his seed and the result is that we who are in Christ are blessed by attribute. This is God's heart towards us. From the beginning His intent was to bless mankind and in fact one of the first things God ever did was to speak blessing over man.

'So God created man in his own image, in the image of God he created him; male and female he created them. [28] God blessed them and said to them, "Be fruitful and increase in number; fill the earth and subdue it. Rule over the fish of the sea and the birds of the air and over every living creature that moves on the ground."'

(Genesis 1:27–28)

(d) Wherever God resides His blessing descends

'When they came to the threshing floor of Nacon, Uzzah reached out and took hold of the ark of God, because the oxen stumbled. [7] The Lord's anger burned against Uzzah because of his irreverent act; therefore God struck him down and he died there beside the ark of God. [8] Then David was angry because the Lord's wrath had broken out against Uzzah, and to this day that place is called Perez Uzzah. [9] David was afraid of the LORD that day and said, "How can the ark of the LORD ever come to me?" [10] He was not willing to take the ark of the LORD to be with him in the City of David. Instead, he took it aside to the house of Obed-Edom the Gittite. [11] The ark of the LORD remained in the house of Obed-Edom the Gittite for three months, and the LORD blessed him and his entire household. [12] Now King David was told, "The LORD has blessed the household of Obed-Edom and everything he has, because of the ark of God." So David went down and brought up the ark of God from the house of Obed-Edom to the City of David with rejoicing. [13] When those who were carrying the ark of the LORD had taken six steps, he sacrificed a bull and a fattened calf. [14] David, wearing a linen ephod, danced before the LORD with all his might, [15] while he and the entire house of Israel brought up the ark of the LORD with shouts and the sound of trumpets. [16] As the ark of the LORD was entering the City of David, Michal daughter of Saul watched from a window. And when she saw King David leaping and dancing before the LORD, she despised him in her heart. [17] They brought the ark of the LORD and set it

> *in its place inside the tent that David had pitched for it, and David sacrificed burnt offerings and fellowship offerings before the LORD.* [18] *After he had finished sacrificing the burnt offerings and fellowship offerings, he blessed the people in the name of the LORD Almighty.'*
>
> (2 Samuel 6:6–18)

Here we see the story of David's attempt to move the ark of the covenant. God struck down Uzzah because he touched the ark. In his panic David left the ark at the house of Obed-Edom the Gittite. The result was that God blessed his home and everything he had. This of course motivated David to retrieve the ark. If God chose to bless Obed-Edom the Gittite's home in this manner while His presence was in an ark made by human hands, how much more will He bless us in whom He lives, temples built not by human effort but by God himself.

(e) God taught His people how to bless

The result of this is that our personalities should in all respects reflect blessing. God taught Moses how to bless and told him to teach Aaron and his sons how to bless the Israelites when they ministered to them

> *'The LORD said to Moses,* [23] *"Tell Aaron and his sons, 'This is how you are to bless the Israelites. Say to them:* [24] *"The LORD bless you and keep you;* [25] *the LORD make his face shine upon you and be gracious to you;* [26] *the LORD turn his face toward you and give you peace."'* [27] *So they will put my name on the Israelites, and I will bless them."'*
>
> (Numbers 6:22–27)

If we choose to bless as God blesses us, then it will become a more noticeable aspect of our personality. We have been recreated 'blessed personalities' and this blessing is not one that anyone can resist. If God says we are blessed no one can rob us of it except ourselves.

We Have Become a Royal Priesthood

As Christians we are 'a royal priesthood'. What do priests do? The answer is they minster. We as believers have a need to minister in many various ways because we have become minsters by rebirth. If we did not minster we could be compared to a football player sitting on the sidelines watching his team play. The moment the opportunity presents itself, instead of playing skilfully, he may play out of his frustration. Sometimes, because we do not get the opportunity to minister to people, we can minister out of frustration if and when the opportunity presents itself. I feel sorry for the weakest member of any group that is not ministering as it should be, because I know that when there are a lot of frustrated believers with no one else to minster to, the weakest member of the group becomes the ministry fodder. In the past I have sometimes felt uncomfortable when faced with individuals who had an overwhelming compulsion to minister. Until recently I did not understand that this desire, though sometimes exercised in an intense manner, was actually natural because, having become *'born again'*, we acquire the status of a royal priesthood.

> *'But you are a chosen people, a **royal priesthood**, a holy nation, a people belonging to God, that you may declare the praises of him who called you out of darkness into his wonderful light.'* (1 Peter 2:9)

One of the functions of a priest is to offer sacrifices, but our sacrifices are not of a redemptive nature. They are spiritual.

> *'Through Jesus, therefore, let us continually offer to God a sacrifice of praise – the fruit of lips that confess his name.* [16] *And do not forget to do good and to share with others, for with such sacrifices God is pleased.'*
> (Hebrews 13:14–16)

Ministry is an aspect of our personality that we need to express in sacrificial praise to God through our lips and all of our actions. If we do not then it will mean that as a priest we will be frustrated and lacking in fulfilment. The essence of the priesthood to which we belong is twofold, firstly praise and secondly the offering up of our bodies as a spiritual sacrifice.

> 'you also, like living stones, are being built into a spiritual house to be a holy priesthood, offering spiritual sacrifices acceptable to God through Jesus Christ.'
> (1 Peter 2:5)

We have become a royal priesthood. Understanding this new aspect of our constitution helps in enhancing ourselves.

We Have Become Disciples of Christ

A disciple of Christ is another aspect to our new position in Christ. I remember when I went to Bible College in Glasgow (BTI), now known as the Glasgow Bible College, a College lecturer said to the whole class on the first day the class studied the subject *doctrines*, 'You are all theologians the day you begin to study the Bible. You will either make good theologians or bad theologians, but whichever, you are now theologians.' I thought this was very profound. Jesus said the same thing using different words.

> 'To the Jews who had believed him, Jesus said, "If you hold to my teaching, you are really my disciples (manthëtës). ^{32} Then you will know the truth, and the truth will set you free." ^{33} They answered him, "We are Abraham's descendants and have never been slaves of anyone. How can you say that we shall be set free?" ^{34} Jesus replied, "I tell you the truth, everyone who sins is a slave to sin. ^{35} Now a slave has no permanent place in the family, but a son belongs to it forever. ^{36} So if the Son sets you free, you will be free indeed. ^{37} I know you are

> *Abraham's descendants. Yet you are ready to kill me, because you have no room for my word."'*
>
> (John 8:31–37)

Jesus said genuine disciples hold to His teaching. The word for disciple that Jesus uses helps us to understand what the nature of a disciple is. The Greek word for disciple used here is the word *'manthëtës'*. It basically means 'learner' because the word originated from the verb *'manthanö'* which means 'to learn'. A disciple is basically one who is in a state of learning. In Jesus' day there were many *'manthëtës'*, like the Pharisees who had their own disciples.

> *'Then the Pharisees went out and laid plans to trap him in his words. ^{16} They sent their disciples to him along with the Herodians. "Teacher," they said, "we know you are a man of integrity and that you teach the way of God in accordance with the truth. You aren't swayed by men, because you pay no attention to who they are."'*
>
> (Matthew 22:14–16)

Even John the Baptist had his own disciples who learned from him (Matthew 11:2–3). We have been called to be disciples of Christ which means we have been called to learners. If we let go of Jesus' teaching then we stop being learners or disciples. Our personalities will stand out for God and can be enhanced only if we remain teachable with regard to the word of God. The minute we think we know it all our personalities become ugly and unattractive. At the point we let go of Jesus' teaching we become deceived and could revert to being slaves of sin, just like Jesus said to those disciples who had also believed in Him (John 8:31–37). People who stand out for God are people who have made a conscious decision to follow Christ regardless of difficulties and to learn from Him in the midst of trials.

> *'Come to me, all you who are weary and burdened, and I will give you rest. ^{29} Take my yoke upon you and learn*

('mathano') *from me, for I am gentle and humble in heart, and you will find rest for your souls.* ³⁰ *For my yoke is easy and my burden is light.'*

(Matthew 11:28–30)

Not all have made a firm commitment to Christ, even though they have believed in Him. After the discourse on Christ being the Bread of Life many disciples left Him as they had not made a firm commitment (John 6:6). If we are going to be individuals whose personalities speak of the glory of God (John 17:22), then we must make a conscious decision to hold to Christ's teaching no matter how difficult it becomes. For instance it is very hard for some people to accept His statement that we must love Him more than our family.

'If anyone comes to me and does not hate his father and mother, his wife and children, his brothers and sisters – yes, even his own life – he cannot be my disciple. ²⁷ *And anyone who does not carry his cross and follow me cannot be my disciple.'* (Luke 14:26–27)

Jesus said some really sharp things here. But unless we really know the heart of God we will not hear what He is really saying. The word that Jesus used here for **'hate'** is the word **'miseo'** which means 'to detest or by extension to love less'. Jesus is not saying hate your family, but He is saying that the place they have in our hearts should be less than the place the Lord has in our hearts. When we compare the love we have for our family to the love we have for our Lord then it should be as if we detest them. He is not actually asking us to hate our family, as this is not the heart of God. A disciple, as far as Jesus is concerned, must put Him first or he cannot be His disciple. Indeed if in any area he is not prepared to take up his cross daily and follow Him he cannot be His disciple. We have by rebirth become disciples of Christ. As a disciple make a firm commitment to study God's word if you want your personality to serve God and be a witness to His name.

A Part of Israel

I have often wondered why I felt such warmth towards Israel. I was amazed but not surprised when I first learned of how they had vanquished their enemies in the six day war. After all they were Israel. I often felt an affinity towards Israel, a sort of kinship. I later understood that is due to believers being of the seed of Abraham.

> *'Therefore, the promise comes by faith, so that it may be by grace and may be guaranteed to all Abraham's offspring – not only to those who are of the law but also to those who are of the faith of Abraham. He is the father of us all.'* (Romans 4:16)

Abraham is not just the father to those who are his biological offspring and descendants, but to all who believe and accept Christ in faith. Abraham is our father because we have put our faith in Christ.

> *'If you belong to Christ, then you are Abraham's seed, and heirs according to the promise.'* (Galatians 3:29)

In Christ we participate in the promise given to Abraham. All of God's promises are answered in Christ and Gentiles come to share in God's covenant promise (2 Corinthians 1:20). But let us understand that not all who are Israelites are actually Abraham's descendants.

> *'It is not as though God's word had failed. For not all who are descended from Israel are Israel. [7] Nor because they are his descendants are they all Abraham's children. On the contrary, "It is through Isaac that your offspring will be reckoned."'* (Romans 9:6–7)

The name Israel is only rightly applied to those Jews who form the saved remnant in Christ (Galatians 6:16). Those Jews who refuse to believe are not descendants.

> *'A man is not a Jew if he is only one outwardly, nor is circumcision merely outward and physical. [29] No, a man is a Jew if he is one inwardly; and circumcision is circumcision of the heart, by the Spirit, not by the written code. Such a man's praise is not from men, but from God.'*
> (Romans 2:28–29)

We Gentiles who have chosen to believe in the Lord Jesus Christ have been grafted on to the Jews who do believe and so we become a part of this Israel of God.

> *'If some of the branches have been broken off, and you, though a wild olive shoot, have been grafted in among the others and now share in the nourishing sap from the olive root, [18] do not boast over those branches. If you do, consider this: You do not support the root, but the root supports you. [19] You will say then, "Branches were broken off so that I could be grafted in." [20] Granted. But they were broken off because of unbelief, and you stand by faith. Do not be arrogant, but be afraid.'*
> (Romans 11:17–20)

We Have Become Members of a Family

I found it very difficult to understand how the people sitting across from me could hold the perspective and view which they held with integrity. We had just finished a long meeting and some people had come back with us to the host's house. This particular couple stayed behind till the end and unfolded their testimony. It became clear that they did not belong to any church because they felt that God had given them a freedom to go to any church they felt like on a Sunday morning. When they said this the scripture came to me:

> *'Let us not give up meeting together, as some are in the habit of doing, but let us encourage one another – and all the more as you see the Day approaching.'*
>
> (Hebrews 10:25)

When I realised that they had no commitment to any local body I was going to challenge them about this, but I realised that they were not actually open to any input into their current circumstance. If our personalities are going to be enhanced for God, then we need to understand that we have become by new birth a part of the family of God. We have a new identity that is wrapped up in family. This new spiritual family that we belong to is similar in its functioning to a human family. Some of the similarities include:
(1) We eat together (1 Corinthians 11:25).
(2) Families help each other (Galatians 6:9–10).
(3) Families have different members:
    (a) Children (Romans 8:16);
    (b) Parents (2 Corinthians 12:14);
    (c) Mothers (1 Timothy 5:1–2);
    (d) Brothers/sisters (1 Timothy 5:2).

> *'The Spirit himself testifies with our spirit that we are God's children.'* (Romans 8:16)

We are the family of God because we have God as our father and we are all sons. To be an individual whose personality stands out for God we must understand that, just as we love and are committed to our earthly family, we ought to be fully committed to God's family. Often people have been hurt by others within the context of a church, and perhaps because they could not cope with sorting out the difficulties they have ended up leaving the church and becoming like the couple I mentioned above – spiritual wanderers, a people who are not committed to any church anywhere.

I understand that sometimes, where there have been difficulties, hurts could have been handled badly, and so an individual may not be able to find security back in the church he has come from. He may also be afraid to become committed to another church. But if an individual has been hurt he has to see it through and genuinely forgive. Family is at the heart of God's desire for us as individuals. That's why He puts us in a family when we are born. It is also why He provides a wife or husband for us and saves us into His family. If you want your personality to be enhanced for God then your gifts and abilities are meant to be used primarily within the context of the family of God.

> *'Now about spiritual gifts, brothers, I do not want you to be ignorant. ^{2} You know that when you were pagans, somehow or other you were influenced and led astray to mute idols. ^{3} Therefore I tell you that no one who is speaking by the Spirit of God says, "Jesus be cursed," and no one can say, "Jesus is Lord," except by the Holy Spirit. ^{4} There are different kinds of gifts, but the same Spirit. ^{5} There are different kinds of service, but the same Lord. ^{6} There are different kinds of working, but the same God works all of them in all men. ^{7} Now to each one the manifestation of the Spirit is given for the common good.'*
> (1 Corinthians 12:1–7)

How can we feel fulfilled or be enhanced in our personality if we are not functioning in the body we have become part of?

> *'Just as each of us has one body with many members, and these members do not all have the same function, ^{5} so in Christ we who are many form one body, and each member belongs to all the others. ^{6} We have different gifts, according to the grace given us. If a man's gift is prophesying, let him use it in proportion to his faith.'*
> (Romans 12:4–6)

Our gifts cannot be utilized in a prominent manner in the church unless the leadership of the church are happy with

Acquired Characteristics

our commitment to church and are sure about the sincerity of our walk with the Lord. It is a silly leader who gives prominent place to an individual who is not committed to church life or willing to give that commitment.

> *'And the things you have heard me say in the presence of many witnesses entrust to **reliable men** who will also be qualified to teach others.'* (2 Timothy 2:2)

If in the appointing of leadership reliability is required then leaders have to look for reliability in every member if they are to be used in any prominent position in church life.

Chapter 8

Developing a Spirit of Excellence

God Wants Us to Excel

God is spoken of in His excellence. He is the excellent God who is second to none. His name is held in great renown throughout the whole world because of His great works.

> *'To the chief Musician upon Gittith, A Psalm of David. O LORD our Lord, how excellent is thy name in all the earth! who hast set thy glory above the heavens.* ^{2} *Out of the mouth of babes and sucklings hast thou ordained strength because of thine enemies, that thou mightest still the enemy and the avenger.* ^{3} *When I consider thy heavens, the work of thy fingers, the moon and the stars, which thou hast ordained;* ^{4} *What is man, that thou art mindful of him? and the son of man, that thou visitest him?'* (Psalm 8:1–4 KJV)

I now find it funny that I used to think, as a Christian, that desiring to excel and be the best was selfish. Now though, I realise that there is a difference between wanting to be and have the best for selfish reasons, compared to wanting to be and have the best for God's glory. **'The image of an object resembles the object'**. A photograph resembles what has been photographed and thus is an image of the object. A mirror reflects the image of a person. *'Excelling should be the natural result of a people created in the image of a God who excels'*. The challenge to excel should not be a thing of fear but a goal set into the heart of man, and the scriptures bear this out.

> *'But just as you excel* ('perisseuo') *in everything – in faith, in speech, in knowledge, in complete earnestness and in your love for us – see that you also excel in this grace of giving. [8] I am not commanding you, but I want to test the sincerity of your love by comparing it with the earnestness of others. [9] For you know the grace of our Lord Jesus Christ, that though he was rich, yet for your sakes he became poor, so that you through his poverty might become rich.'* (2 Corinthians 8:7–9)

The Greek word used to express *'excelling'* here is the word *'perisseuo'*. It carries with it the idea of lavishly abounding (in quantity or quality). It means 'to abound, to have more, to be more abundant, to excel'. The fact is that God wants us to excel in everything in this life. There should be no area in which we should not be seeking to excel whether in labour, business, study, preaching, ministry or even pleasure. All should be done to the glory of God.

There are many areas in which God wants us to excel that we could look at, but we could not possibly do them all justice in this book. But we will look at three foundational areas and one general one that are helpful to the enhancement of personality. Our attitude towards excelling is basically our disposition towards it. If that attitude is fear then how can we ever achieve the best, because fear paralyses? Rather because the scriptures encourage us to seek to have excellence in everything we should aim to abound as an example to everyone around us. If the attitude is right and the same as that of Christ Jesus (Philippians 2) then seeking to excel or to have an abundance of faith, speech, knowledge (etc.) is not wrong and should be pursued as it will gain us respect in our homes and communities. *'Like God those who excel have an excellent name'*.

If you have been taught not to seek to be the best, or if you have been taught that seeking to be the best is the same thing as trying to be better than someone else, then you will find it hard to want to excel. Liberty from this frame of mind comes by accepting the word of God on this issue. As long as our attitude is the same as Jesus then it is not wrong to want to be the best for God. *'The deeds of those who excel outshine the deeds of those who do not'*. John the Baptist had a large following and his holy life outshone the lives of the Pharisees and Sadducees. His respect impacted everyone in Israel from the streets to the palace. He excelled in his preaching of repentance and his deeds outshone the religious rulers of his day.

I remember when I was a young man at secondary school in Lagos (Nigeria). We had state selection trials for the one hundred meters sprint. I watched in disbelief as one young man crossed the finishing tape while the rest were still half way down the track. The whole stadium full of young teenagers erupted in rapturous applause because that young man had excelled. His deed had outshone everyone else on the track. The Governor of the state immediately offered him a state scholarship which was the reward that was promised to the overall winner.

Jesus also excelled. When He came along John the Baptist said of Him that He must increase and I must decease. He did not say this meaning he should now stop preaching repentance or stop serving God. He said this because he knew that the glory of the Messiah would outshine his because the deeds of the Messiah would be more excellent and thus gain Him a higher name. This does not mean that John the Baptist was in any way mediocre or irrelevant, rather he was the greatest man of his times until Jesus came along. No-one's actions can be surmised by anyone else as being irrelevant or meaningless or less important than someone else's. Only God can judge whether our deeds are significant or not. A roadsweeper who walks in obedience with

God all his life gains a better name in the sight of God than a great evangelist who walks in disobedience most of his life. John the Baptist was not in competition with Jesus. *'As individuals we are not in competition with anyone else, we are only in competition with ourselves'*. The example of John was not meant to illustrate that one man can be better than another, as that is impossible, but it is meant to illustrate that our deeds, however small scale or large scale, however discreet or prominent, will gain an excellent name for us. We do not aim to be the best at the expense of anyone else, nor for the feeding of our pride, but for the glory of God. Even our thought life is to be caught up with those things that are excellent.

> *'Finally, brothers, whatever is true, whatever is noble, whatever is right, whatever is pure, whatever is lovely, whatever is admirable – if anything is excellent or praiseworthy – think about such things.'* (Philippians 4:8)

(a) Excelling in personal spirituality

God gives us the Holy Spirit and the gifts of the Spirit for several reasons, one of which is for the benefit of the Church, and so we are to excel in spirituality.

> *'So it is with you. Since you are eager to have spiritual gifts, try to excel* ('perisseuo') *in gifts that build up the church.'* (1 Corinthians 14:12)

The word here is the Greek word *'perisseuo'* which means *'to abound'*. God wants us to have an abundance of the Holy Spirit. All excelling must stem from the work of the Spirit in our lives and not from the flesh or the soul. Human effort will be effective for a while but can not attain the goals set out by the Spirit. Not only is it a waste of time trying to excel in the flesh for the Christian, it is sinful if the Holy Spirit has no part in what the flesh is trying to achieve. The flesh cannot save and the soul will lead us astray (Galatians 3:3–5). God wants our personalties to abound and shine out spiritually. But what is spirituality? Spirituality is present in other religions. For instance a lot of people consider Ghandi to be a spiritual man, and yes, he was spiritual but not through the Holy Spirit.

> *'Dear friends, do not believe every spirit, but test the spirits to see whether they are from God, because many false prophets have gone out into the world. ^{2} This is how you can recognize the Spirit of God: Every spirit that acknowledges that Jesus Christ has come in the flesh is from God.'* (1 John 4:1–2)

Being spiritual means being concerned with a spirit in the sense of the supernatural. We can tell if our personalties are spiritual in the right sense if we measure it against the work of the Holy Spirit. The Holy Spirit is concerned with bringing to mind the word of God which is also called the Sword of the Spirit. Abounding or excelling in the Spirit will mean abounding in the word of God, which we cover in chapter 5 – 'Acquiring a Faith-Filled Personality'. Excellence in the utilization of the word will only be found through the help of the Spirit. It is His Sword after all.

> *'But when he, the Spirit of truth, comes, he will guide you into all truth. He will not speak on his own; he will speak only what he hears, and he will tell you what is yet to come.'* (John 16:13)

If we are being spiritual in the right way then we will take on the characteristics of the Holy Spirit and acquire a personality that in part reflects Him. A personality that is lacking in these things ought to reconsider his walk and allow the Spirit to help him bear such fruit in his life. Just as a fruit tree grows and bears fruit so, as we keep in step with the Spirit of God, He bears abundant excellent fruit in our lives. He desires to help us abound.

> *'But the fruit of the Spirit is love, joy, peace, patience, kindness, goodness, faithfulness ('pistis' – faith), [23] gentleness and self-control. Against such things there is no law. [24] Those who belong to Christ Jesus have crucified the sinful nature with its passions and desires. [25] Since we live by the Spirit, let us keep in step with the Spirit.'*
>
> (Galatians 5:22–25)

In the past when people have written books on temperament, they have rightly highlighted the need to develop these fruits in our lives. Unfortunately, many have limited personality to temperament. As you are discovering, personality is much wider than temperament. Expressing the temperament of the Spirit is only half of the coin, the other side is the manifestation of the power of the Spirit. This is what Jesus did. He accredited His power and spirituality to the work of the Holy Spirit in His life, saying it was the Spirit of the Lord that was upon Him (Luke 4:18–19). If we want to excel in spirituality we ought to ask ourselves the question, 'how much of the character and power of the Spirit am I manifesting?'.

> *'Now to each one the manifestation of the Spirit is given for the common good. [8] To one there is given through the Spirit the message of wisdom, to another the message of knowledge by means of the same Spirit, [9] to another faith by the same Spirit, to another gifts of healing by that one Spirit, [10] to another miraculous powers, to another prophecy, to another distinguishing between spirits, to another speaking in different kinds of tongues, and to still another the interpretation of tongues. [11] All these are the work of one and the same Spirit, and he gives them to each one, just as he determines.'*
>
> (1 Corinthians 12:7–11)

Spiritual gifts are given for the common good of the whole assembly. If we are manifesting the power of the Spirit we are being spiritual. Our very competence can and will only come from the Holy Spirit if it is to count for eternity. We should actively cultivate the work of the Spirit in our lives.

> *'He has made us competent as ministers of a new covenant – not of the letter but of the Spirit; for the letter kills, but the Spirit gives life.'* (2 Corinthians 3:6)

The Holy Spirit will transform us into the likeness of Christ (2 Corinthians 3:17–18). For those of us who want personalties that stand out for God, excelling in the things of the Spirit is an important priority, and God is willing to give to us more of His Spirit without limit if we ask.

> *'Which of you fathers, if your son asks for a fish, will give him a snake instead?* [12] *Or if he asks for an egg, will give him a scorpion?* [13] *If you then, though you are evil, know how to give good gifts to your children, how much more will your Father in heaven give the Holy Spirit to those who ask him!'* (Luke 11:11–13)

(b) Excellence in personal sexuality

Foundational to being able to excel in personality is understanding the importance of sexuality. Sexuality is intrinsic to our personality. If we chose to allow our sexuality to be enhanced for God it is a beautiful thing. I have met some couples who have excellent marriages. I have at times felt convicted because some of the men could be classified as the stereotype gentlemen, not weak, soft or wimpish, but real men, full of the Holy Spirit, and yet gentle. Often their wives have confirmed that they excel in most aspects of marriage. This is what happens when a man seeks to excel in his sexuality. I thought about this for a while and realised that everyone of us can excel as individuals whether we are married or single. **'Excelling in sexuality is excelling in what it means to be a man or what it means to be a woman'.**

Enhancing Your Personality for God

(i) The joy of singleness

God has called us as individuals to live within certain constraints and relationships. There is nothing wrong with being single as a Christian, nor does being single mean one has to disregard one's sexuality. The problem is that most people equate sexuality with sex, or sex appeal. Sexuality is much more complicated than that. **'Your sexuality is that which has been written into your genes at creation'**. A single person must be a good steward of his sexuality with the same degree of care that a married person must. Marriage is not the be all and end all of life. Yes it is good to get married to the right partner, but from what I have seen in counselling, for many people it is a nightmare to be hitched to the wrong partner. Single Christians frequently feel that they cannot achieve much as a single, but this is not true. Remember, Jesus was not married and He was the most perfect human being that walked the face of the earth. Being single did not limit Him in any respect. Jesus excelled in what it means to be a man. The fact that He had no sexual relationships did not limit Him from excelling in what it means to be male. Often the world sends out the image that to be whole as a person or to express sexuality means to have sex. It conjures up the image that says you cannot possibly be fulfilled in your sexuality without the act of procreation. This kind of wrong approach to the stewardship of sexuality has meant that now in Britain one out of three marriages ends in divorce (according to some estimates). Sexuality is meant to be expressed within the context of a God-centred life built on God's word and principles. For singles the advantages of being sexually inactive until marriage are incalculable. Celibacy gives opportunity for single-minded investment in ministry for Christ.

> *'I would like you to be free from concern. An unmarried man is concerned about the Lord's affairs – how he can please the Lord.* [33] *But a married man is concerned about the affairs of this world – how he can please his wife –* [34] *and his interests are divided. An unmarried woman or*

> *virgin is concerned about the Lord's affairs: Her aim is to be devoted to the Lord in both body and spirit. But a married woman is concerned about the affairs of this world – how she can please her husband.* ³⁵ *I am saying this for your own good, not to restrict you, but that you may live in a right way in undivided devotion to the Lord.'*
> (1 Corinthians 7:32–35)

We should all be sexually inactive, and in that sense celibate, until we get married as an act of obedience to the Lord. God created us to function within committed relationships and denying ourselves is an investment worth making. **'Every investment brings forth its own reward'**. To invest your sexuality in God's will certainly secures its own reward because God has promised to repay us for such commitment unto Him.

> *'"I tell you the truth," Jesus replied, "no one who has left home or brothers or sisters or mother or father or children or fields for me and the gospel* ³⁰ *will fail to receive a hundred times as much in this present age (homes, brothers, sisters, mothers, children and fields – and with them, persecutions) and in the age to come, eternal life."'*
> (Mark 10:29–30)

Not only do we benefit by having a pure marriage bed, without the many complications that can arise out of sexual sin before marriage, but the Lord will most definitely ensure that we have a family around us if we are single-mindedly devoted to Him. Sometimes this will mean finding a spouse, while at other times it will mean being single but we will be given Christian family to relate to. If your desire is to get married then it is probably true to say that God does not want you to be single, and will find you a partner, but while the partner tarries we have an obligation to use our singleness to serve God. We need to train ourselves up until we excel in what it means to be a singe man or a single woman.

> 'For the LORD God is a sun and shield; the LORD bestows favour and honour; no good thing does he withhold from those whose walk is blameless.' (Psalm 84:11)

(ii) The significance of sexuality

The context that the Holy Spirit wants to work within is the context in which He created us. Into every cell in our body God has written the fact that we are either male or female. However some individuals try to deny their personality. We all know of young ladies and mature women who, through dislike of their femininity, have taken to dressing like boys or men, and young and mature men who, through dislike of their masculinity, have taken to dressing like young ladies or mature women. This is a shame. God has made us unique and desires us to express that uniqueness within the context of our maleness or femaleness. Your personality cannot excel for God if you are ashamed of your sexuality.

The tendency today is to stress the equality of men and women while at the same time debase the particular importance of our maleness or femaleness. When an individual attempts to camouflage his gender by wearing clothes that obscure his gender because he does not like his sexuality, then this aspect of gender obscuring is simply the external manifestation of an inward problem. The reasons why women have acted more like men are understandable. They have over many centuries been subject to a catalogue of abuse and subjection. Consequently many have thought that the only way to overturn such prejudice was to become like men in every way possible. Though it is right to stand up for equality it is a shame that many women are having to do it by blurring what they have been gloriously created in the first place – *'women'*. The eradication of injustices to women cannot be achieved by ignoring and degrading our gender. We can never really know who we are if we are not being true to ourselves by denying our sexuality.

The differences in sexuality are there in order that we can best fulfil the role God has for us in our life. Just like one is gifted to be able to play the piano and another is intellectually gifted so that he or she can become a doctor, it is wrong to think of equality as meaning we can all have the same roles in life. A man can not be a woman any more than a woman can be a man. We are not all equal financially, nor are we all equal in artistic gifting or talents, yet we do not consider these differences to be an indication of inferiority. In the Lord's eyes we have equality in terms of value, dignity and worth, regardless of gender. We should not allow the world or the Devil to convince us that gender is a hindrance to serving God.

> *'The LORD God said, "It is not good for the man to be alone. I will make a helper suitable for him."*
>
> (Genesis 2:18)

At the very heart of the role of women is the desire to work in relation to their husbands as help mates. This is not some subordinate role (Ephesians 5), rather the role is a glorious position given by God Himself. Men also have a role within marriage which is not one of superiority but of love and responsibility. Our roles in life are central to our personality and are based on our sexuality.

Often women feel that they are excluded from many things that men can do, but this is not so. Proverbs 31 shows us that women have a special place in the home. It shows that a hard working wife can best achieve within the context of the role God created her to live in, firstly a woman, then a wife, and then a working mother.

> *'A wife of noble character who can find? She is worth far more than rubies. [11] Her husband has full confidence in her and lacks nothing of value. [12] She brings him good, not harm, all the days of her life. [13] She selects wool and flax and works with eager hands. [14] She is like the merchant ships, bringing her food from afar. [15] She gets up while it is still dark; she provides food for her family and portions for her servant girls. [16] She considers a field and buys it; out of her earnings she plants a vineyard.*

17 She sets about her work vigorously; her arms are strong for her tasks. 18 She sees that her trading is profitable, and her lamp does not go out at night. 19 In her hand she holds the distaff and grasps the spindle with her fingers. 20 She opens her arms to the poor and extends her hands to the needy.' (Proverbs 31:10–20)

It appears to me that the kind of woman being spoken of in Proverbs is not only hard working, she appears to be able to do as much as any man. The most important thing, though, is that everything she does is not at the expense of what God has made her. On the contrary her role as a wife is pivotal to everything she does. Roles are important. Some women, knowing that they could achieve more in life, have felt the need to discard their femininity in order to do this. As a Christian you don't have to compromise your sexuality in order to be successful, rather, the individual will be more successful if such an individual is not denying the truth about himself, whatever aspect of his or her personality is considered to be a hindrance. Denying individual sexuality will lead to wrong patterns in marriage and wrong and abnormal sexual relationships.

(c) Excellence in personal work
Our attitude towards work or business could leave us with the feeling that it is either a blessing or a curse. Our perspective of work will shape our attitude towards it. A person may be relaxed, though he enjoys a heavy workload, or feel he is working though trying to relax, depending on his perspective. For instance, if while he is playing a game of tennis he is frantically thinking of how he is going to win the game his play will be like hard work. On the other hand if a mechanic finishes his shift, goes home, and starts to work on a sports car he is building from scratch, he will not feel he is working. Because he is relaxed he does not regard it as work but as a hobby. Our attitude counts a great deal towards our approach to work. There is no point denying that work can have its negative aspects. The dark side of toil can be seen in

the Hebrew words translated *'work'*. *'Amal'*, for instance, means 'labour, toil or trouble'. It recognises the fact that work can be unpleasant and frustrating drudgery that never produces satisfactory profit.

> *'But the Egyptians mistreated us and made us suffer, putting us to hard labour. ⁷ Then we cried out to the LORD, the God of our fathers, and the LORD heard our voice and saw our misery, toil* ('amal') *and oppression. ⁸ So the LORD brought us out of Egypt with a mighty hand and an outstretched arm, with great terror and with miraculous signs and wonders.'* (Deuteronomy 26:6-8)

This word is often used in Scripture to speak of work that is painful and tiresome. Other words highlight different aspects of work. People live in a world that has been tainted with sin. Man struggles to produce a yield from the land. Nevertheless it can be productive and satisfying if given to God. In the Old Testament God is understood with respect to the work He has done. He is a God who is described as never slumbering when needed. God's works give Him everlasting praise (Psalm 145:4, 9-10). They declare His righteousness (Psalm 145:17) and bring Him joy (Psalm 104:31). His works are evidence of His supreme power, authority, wisdom and might. Moses understood God's works as revealing His distinctiveness from other gods.

> *'O Sovereign LORD, you have begun to show to your servant your greatness and your strong hand. For what god is there in heaven or on earth who can do the deeds and mighty works you do?'* (Deuteronomy 3:24)

Just like God, men through work can achieve things that bring great satisfaction, value and significance, because this God who works hard and successfully accomplishes much, expects His creation to work hard and bear fruit.

> *'Then God said, "Let the land produce vegetation: seed-bearing plants and trees on the land that bear ('asah') fruit with seed in it, according to their various kinds." And it was so.'* (Genesis 1:11)

'Asah' means 'to accomplish and be busy'. Adam was created to fit into a context of work and friendship with God. Whilst Adam found satisfaction in his work prior to the fall, his sin was responsible for introducing the negative aspect to work.

> *'To Adam he said, "Because you listened to your wife and ate from the tree about which I commanded you, 'You must not eat of it,' Cursed is the ground because of you; through painful toil you will eat of it all the days of your life. ^{18} It will produce thorns and thistles for you, and you will eat the plants of the field. ^{19} By the sweat of your brow you will eat your food until you return to the ground, since from it you were taken; for dust you are and to dust you will return."'* (Genesis 3:17–19)

But despite all of the negative aspects to work it is a divine provision and expectation.

> *'Go to the ant, you sluggard; consider its ways and be wise! ^{7} It has no commander, no overseer or ruler, ^{8} yet it stores its provisions in summer and gathers its food at harvest. ^{9} How long will you lie there, you sluggard? When will you get up from your sleep? ^{10} A little sleep, a little slumber, a little folding of the hands to rest – ^{11} and poverty will come on you like a bandit and scarcity like an armed man.'* (Proverbs 6:6–11)

From the pattern derived from God it is seen that work affects not only the person working but also those around him. A man's work will bring to him more than just the provision of physical needs. The product of our labours can either bring glory to God in a way similar to the works of

His hands or a man's labours can witness against us just as the idols made by the people of God witnessed against them.

God constantly warns against oppressing the worker. He detests dishonest scales. There is nothing wrong with being prosperous, but to become prosperous at the expense of others is evil. We encounter such attitudes in the book of Acts (chapter 16) which describes the exploitation of a girl who was possessed of a spirit of fortune telling. Luke 19 deals directly with work. Here Jesus tells of the master who left his servants with capital to invest. They were told to put the money to work until their master came back. Clearly work is associated with earning a profit, and this is commended by Jesus in the parable. It is not wrong to chase a profit but as with all things the businessman's attitude about his plans must always take the Lord's will into account.

> *'Now listen, you who say, "Today or tomorrow we will go to this or that city, spend a year there, carry on business and make money."* ^{14} *Why, you do not even know what will happen tomorrow. What is your life? You are a mist that appears for a little while and then vanishes.* ^{15} *Instead, you ought to say, "If it is the Lord's will, we will live and do this or that."* ^{16} *As it is, you boast and brag. All such boasting is evil.* ^{17} *Anyone, then, who knows the good he ought to do and doesn't do it, sins.'*
>
> (James 4:13–17)

Paul worked to set an example in the churches. Idleness or dependence on others is not a godly trait for people who can work because believers are not to burden others (2 Thessalonians 3:6–15).

The outlook for the compliant believer is very encouraging. It enables him or her to contribute to the well-being of others. Those who undertake special work for the Lord are to be esteemed.

> *'Now we ask you, brothers, to respect those who work hard among you, who are over you in the Lord and who admonish you. [13] Hold them in the highest regard in love because of their work. Live in peace with each other.'*
>
> (1 Thessalonians 5:12–13)

The benefit of aiming for excellence is seen in the end product of our labour. If we have excellence as one of our motivations there will be a multiplication in our output. When people become involved in working toward a goal, motivation is always a matter of concern. Our feeling about our work will affect how well we work. But feelings must not dictate to us about our work. Again this underlines why the will has to be seated in the spiritual rather than in the soulish realm.

Goal setting is highly desirable for the Christian worker. As long as they are scripturally acceptable, goals that stretch us are exciting. In our work we ought to set ourselves goals that are clearly defined. People often do not set clear goals because they are afraid of failing to achieve their goals. The point of goal setting for the Christian should be to try to achieve more than you possibly could naturally. We have the Holy Spirit directing, motivating and helping us. The effects of setting goals on our achievements can be staggering.

When we begin to struggle in our work though illness or other reasons the effects it can have on the family are often disastrous. Because work plays such a central role to daily living, problems associated with work can have devastating consequences on the family unit, one important reason for setting aside a good insurance policy, whether you are self-employed or not. Good stewardship means protecting your family the best you can and then in faith leaving the rest to God. Some Christians would wrongly consider an insurance policy as an indication of lack of faith. I have met some widows who have had reason to thank God that their husbands adequately provided for them. Provision for your family in time of crisis is not an optional extra, it should be a high priority. Even a policy with just a few pence a week is better than none if you can get it.

(ii) Workaholics and work

Some struggle in work because they are workaholics. A workaholic is a person who is compulsively addicted to his or her job. Such persons work for work's sake. It is an illness that sees no viable alternative to work. No other activity that can use so much energy demands such attention, provides habitual sociable interaction and a sellable service or product to boot. Most workaholics are not happy with their lives, though some are. Work can take on such significance if it is an anxiety coping strategy, much like a child sucking his thumb, if it is seen as a substitute for family and friends. Certain attitudes such as poor self-image, rigidity, disturbed interpersonal relationships, characterize these people. The person who is cheerful about his work, takes an active role in his work *and* if he also takes an active role in his family, is usually a healthy individual. But the person who is pessimistic and believes he has little control over his life is a much more significant health risk and more prone to burn out. Unfortunately the workaholic usually places his family at a lower priority than his work. Some workaholics avoid the demands of family and domestic duties under the guise of providing a better life style for their loved ones. The lack of a loving nurturing father or mother can affect a child's ability to love or feel loved by God or other persons. What the child needs is quality time even if the child cannot get a great deal of time.

The only cure for stress is repentance. Most problems related to work addiction are stress-related illnesses. The cure for the workaholic must involve an acceptance and understanding that because he has made work his overriding priority, it has consequences for both him and his family. He needs to recognise that even with work Jesus must be Lord and his family must come first.

In conclusion it can be said that work is best enjoyed when it is the rendering of wilful obedience to the Lord Jesus

Christ. When we desire to excel for God's sake then we will take time to rest. Like King David who worshipped God as he tended his fathers sheep, we ought to worship God in our work and not worship our work. If we choose to worship God in our work then the drudgery and pain of work will be replaced by joy.

In light of the scriptural evidence I perceive that God intended work to be a joy rather than a burden. Work was never meant to be a heavy yoke which was unbearable, but rather God-appointed and inspired. Just as Adam was given work to do so God has work for all of us.

(d) Excellency in personal giving

God also wants us to excel in our sacrificial giving. Abel is spoken of in the scriptures as pleasing God because he excelled in his giving to God.

> 'By faith Abel offered unto God a more excellent sacrifice than Cain, by which he obtained witness that he was righteous, God testifying of his gifts: and by it he being dead yet speaketh.' (Hebrews 11:4 KJV)

Excelling in giving God the best is one of the most beautiful acts of love we can ever hope to undertake. Giving Him second best is not an act of love towards God. Jesus said we must love God with all that is within us.

> '"Teacher, which is the greatest commandment in the Law?" [37] Jesus replied: "Love the Lord your God with all your heart and with all your soul and with all your mind."' (Matthew 22:36–37)

Real love is expressed in what we do, not just what we say. If what we do is a reflection of our love then what we give to God is also a reflection of that same love. If we are going to develop excellence in our personality then we need to make sure that what we are giving costs us something like it cost Abel, or the widow who gave her all.

Developing a Spirit of Excellence

> '*Calling his disciples to him, Jesus said, "I tell you the truth, this poor widow has put more into the treasury than all the others. ⁴⁴ They all gave out of their wealth; but she, out of her poverty, put in everything – all she had to live on."*' (Mark 12:43–44)

I remember visiting one pastor's house and was amazed to see the gates open up electrically. In addition to pastoring he was also a highly successful practitioner. His house was beautifully decorated with the finest and the best. I thought about many people whom I knew would have great difficulty with such extravagance. But I said nothing. Later on as we spoke I found out that this man gave nothing but the best to the church. He believed that the church building, for instance, should have nothing but the best decorations and I was told that it was better decorated than his own house. Recently he had fitted a £14,000 speaker system into the church. This might sound extravagant but I believe he was a man who gave of his best to God no matter what it cost. He was in pursuit of excellence and his actions bore it out just like the widow who gave her two mites. Holding lightly the things God gives to us is the best policy; possessions, though wonderful to have, become a snare when we hold on to them too tightly or go after them covetously.

> '*Then he said to them, "Watch out! Be on your guard against all kinds of greed; a man's life does not consist in the abundance of his possessions."*' (Luke 12:15)

Conclusion

Whatever the area of excellence the goal is a personality that can be spoken of in the same manner in which Doctor Luke could speak of Theophilus. Both the gospel of Luke and the book of Acts were written to him. Whatever our station in life or whatever our call our desire should be to be the best. Solomon was one such figure who excelled in his position as king.

> *'King Solomon was greater in riches and wisdom than all the other kings of the earth. ^{24} The whole world sought audience with Solomon to hear the wisdom God had put in his heart. ^{25} Year after year, everyone who came brought a gift – articles of silver and gold, robes, weapons and spices, and horses and mules.'*
>
> (1 Kings 10:23–25)

The reason why he prospered and excelled was simple. When he had a chance to have whatever he wanted he was selfless in his request. He wanted to give of his best in serving God's people and so God gave him even more than he asked for.

> *'Give me wisdom and knowledge, that I may lead this people, for who is able to govern this great people of yours?'* (2 Chronicles 1:10)

God gave him riches in addition to all his wisdom. Solomon did not squander his opportunities. He so excelled that he became the greatest King in the world second to none. We can become the greatest at whatever God has called us to do whether it is plumbing, building, gardening or even evangelism as each one of us has a unique plan in God's purposes.

Chapter 9

Personality and Appearance

(by Yinka and Fiona Oyekan)

(a) Starting from Inside Out

The way we look is vitally important to us all. Men and women alike want to look good. There are many kinds of help available. Women's magazines are particulary full of it, and there must be thousands if not millions of diets to try. If success is not achieved then advice is given on what clothes to wear to disguise the parts you don't like. Some in the quest for beauty will go to the extent of having cosmetic surgery. We all want to be beautiful or handsome because we want to feel approved of, and accepted. Wives seek to look their best for their husbands, and so dress to please because they love them. I listened to Fiona explaining this at a women's rally.

> *'We want to please others, usually people we care about. My husband has certain tastes and dislikes in clothing and make-up that are not always what I would choose, but because I love him and want to please him, and as long as I don't absolutely hate what he likes, I usually lean more to what pleases him ... We want to look beautiful because we want to feel confident and good about ourselves...'*

Of course I know as a man that this is also true for me. I tend to dress to please Fiona, but also because I do feel good about myself when I am not too scruffy. Our outer appearance is something that is vitally important to us and so we should discipline ourselves in presenting a favourable image.

But what emphasis should we put on outer beauty? Fiona put this outward aspect of our personality into context.

> *'The thing about all the helps to a better appearance is that sometimes what we see on the outside is not always what is going on inside. People often put on a happy face when inside they feel very sad. Sometimes people put on a hard face that says "stay away, I can look after myself". Your external appearance may be the most important thing to some, but you can't always judge by appearance.'*

If we make outward appearance the measure by which we judge people we will make mistakes, hopefully not costly ones. Samuel made an attempt to guess who the Lord would chose as king over Israel.

> *'Samuel replied, "Yes, in peace; I have come to sacrifice to the LORD. Consecrate yourselves and come to the sacrifice with me." Then he consecrated Jesse and his sons and invited them to the sacrifice. ⁶ When they arrived, Samuel saw Eliab and thought, "Surely the Lord's anointed stands here before the LORD." ⁷ But the LORD said to Samuel, "Do not consider his appearance or his height, for I have rejected him. The LORD does not look at the things man looks at. Man looks at the outward appearance, but the LORD looks at the heart." ⁸ Then Jesse called Abinadab and had him pass in front of Samuel. But Samuel said, "The LORD has not chosen this one either." ⁹ Jesse then had Shammah pass by, but Samuel said, "Nor has the LORD chosen this one." ¹⁰ Jesse had seven of his sons pass before Samuel, but Samuel said to him, "The LORD has not chosen these."*

> ¹¹ *So he asked Jesse, "Are these all the sons you have?" "There is still the youngest," Jesse answered, "but he is tending the sheep." Samuel said, "Send for him; we will not sit down until he arrives."* ¹² *So he sent and had him brought in. He was ruddy, with a fine appearance and handsome features. Then the LORD said, "Rise and anoint him; he is the one."'* (1 Samuel 16:4–12)

Samuel was initially impressed by the appearance of Eliab but he was not the chosen one. It drew a sharp rebuke and reminder that God looks at the heart, not the external appearance. Jesus intimated that externals can deceive if we are not careful.

> '*Woe to you, teachers of the law and Pharisees, you hypocrites! You are like whitewashed tombs, which look beautiful on the outside but on the inside are full of dead men's bones and everything unclean.* ²⁸ *In the same way, on the outside you appear to people as righteous but on the inside you are full of hypocrisy and wickedness.*' (Matthew 23:27–28)

He was basically saying that what they **'*appeared*'** to be was not what they were. **'*All that glitters is not gold*'**, and so believers ought to learn like Paul how to consider people, but not because of their appearance.

> '*As for those who seemed to be important – whatever they were makes no difference to me; God does not judge by external appearance* ('prospon') *– those men added nothing to my message.*' (Galatians 2:6)

The word for **'*appearance*'** used here is the word **'*prospon*'** which means **'*appearance, person or countenance*'**. The inference that we have to take from Paul's statement is, if God does not judge by appearances we should not judge by externals either. What we see before us is not the whole person, just the outward aspect.

Enhancing Your Personality for God

But can this external be enhanced anyway? Fiona commented on this in the ladies rally.

> *'It may matter to people whether you have large eyes or small eyes or if you prefer to wear make-up or not, but what matters to God is if you are beautiful on the inside. Inner beauty is the only kind of beauty that lasts and it only comes from God.'*

Moses acquired this kind of external glory which came directly from a revelation of the Lord. Having spent many days with the Lord he came down from the mountain and his face shone so brightly that he had to wear a veil.

> 'When Moses came down from Mount Sinai with the two tablets of the Testimony in his hands, he was not aware that his face was radiant because he had spoken with the LORD. ^{30} When Aaron and all the Israelites saw Moses, his face was radiant, and they were afraid to come near him.' (Exodus 34:29–30)

Paul says of this that if such was the ministry of the Old Covenant, how shall not the ministry of the Spirit be much more glorious? The Holy Spirit will do such a work within us that will mean fruit will develop on the inside and not the other way round.

> 'Your beauty should not come from outward adornment, such as braided hair and the wearing of gold jewellery and fine clothes. ^{4} Instead, it should be that of your inner self, the unfading beauty of a gentle and quiet spirit, which is of great worth in God's sight.' (1 Peter 3:3–4)

If we want to enhance our personality for God, our outward appearance is important, but only in that it is enhanced from an encounter with God. Real beauty or handsomeness comes from the work of the Spirit on the inside of a believer. It is not what ladies put on their face or the calibre of a man's grooming.

(b) How Do We Get This Kind of Beauty?

The enhancement of our looks must come from encounters with God in which we, the created, yield to the creator. I can remember incidents where a nice young boy or girl seemed like lovely children until they opened their mouth. I have often been amazed at the level of foul language which can proceed from the lips of a child who appears very innocent. Often it has made me think of the child as not very nice, pretty or handsome after all. At the ladies rally that Fiona was speaking at she indicated the only barrier to this supernatural beauty which can be acquired is sin. She said:

> *'How do we get this kind of beauty? Can every one have it? Yes, everyone can have it if they want it, but there is one thing in the way. Only one thing can stop us from having the kind of beauty that pleases God and this is called sin. To be clean and beautiful in God's eyes we have to get rid of sin. Sin separates us from God and makes us ugly in His eyes. Things like jealousy of another person, being envious of what people have, anger and unforgiveness in our hearts towards people who have hurt us or family that has rejected us makes us ugly. Even little white lies make us ugly. Many people also find that though they momentarily feel good whilst gossiping about someone they ultimately feel bad about themselves in the long run.'*

Like some little children who open their mouths only to disappoint the hearer because of the bad language, what is within an adult or individual comes out of us, and if these things are not good then it makes us look ugly.

> *'For from within, out of men's hearts, come evil thoughts, sexual immorality, theft, murder, adultery,* [22] *greed,*

> *malice, deceit, lewdness, envy, slander, arrogance and folly.* ²³ *All these evils come from inside and make a man "unclean".'*
>
> (Mark 7:21–23)

Tommy was a man who walked around with a frown on his face. He had a great deal of resentment that he felt against his parents whom he believed did not really love him. He was a handsome young man who should have been optimistic about his future. But this resentment was like a cancer within him which permeated his whole being including how he looked. His countenance was completely downcast. Unless Tommy rids himself of this resentment it will continue to affect his appearance and self-esteem. Mary was another individual who had a rather pleasant temperament. She appeared to be as sweet as pie, but the moment her husband was mentioned she poured out an angry tirade of sarcastic abuse towards him, even though he was dead. Her face would contort and twist, reflecting her feelings towards him. She had not forgiven him for dying before her. Though, unlike Tommy, her bitterness was deep set it did surface from time to time, and when it did it made her look ugly.

If sin in the form of anger, bitterness and the like is not dealt with and repented of, it will cause the individual to look ugly. **'Sin is like a cancer that corrupts every facet of our personality, making us ugly'.** Thus dealing with sin is the first important consideration for every individual who wants to enhance their appearance for God.

(c) Taming the Flesh

> *'Wherein in time past ye walked according to the course of this world, according to the prince of the power of the air, the spirit that now worketh in the children of disobedience:* ³ *Among whom also we all had our conversation in times past in the lusts of our flesh, fulfilling the desires of the flesh and of the mind; and were by nature the children of wrath, even as others.'*
>
> (Ephesians 2:2–3)

Personality and Appearance

We need to ensure, if we want to enhance our personality for God, that our bodies are not dictating to us, but that the Holy Spirit does indeed have pre-eminence in our lives. There are several ways of bringing the flesh under control of the Spirit. One way is fasting. ***'What you feed is what grows'.*** If you feed the spirit of a man the man's spirit grows. If you feed the flesh the flesh grows in strength. Thus fasting is one way of keeping the body under control. Another way of taming the body is to keep fit. Some individuals, through lack of exercise, develop a slothfulness that hinders their ability to serve God. Laziness is best combated by keeping ourselves occupied and fit.

Appendix

The Problem of Sin

Sin is what separates us from God and it started in the Garden of Eden when Adam and Eve disobeyed God. The consequence of their sin was separation from God and this still remains the consequence today.

The Temptation

> *'"You will not surely die," the serpent said to the woman.* [5] *"For God knows that when you eat of it your eyes will be opened, and you will be like God, knowing good and evil."* [6] *When the woman saw that the fruit of the tree was good for food and pleasing to the eye, and also desirable for gaining wisdom, she took some and ate it. She also gave some to her husband, who was with her, and he ate it.'* (Genesis 3:4–6)

We all know what sin is, even when we are not told what it is. This is because our consciences tell us. When we are doing something wrong, we feel guilty. The Bible shows us that **Adam was in fact not deceived. He knew what he was doing** (1 Timothy 2:14). **The Devil played to their pride**, and this is what he still does today. He knows that mankind is proud and seeks to appeal to that pride.

> *'For God knows that when you eat of it your eyes will be opened, and you will be like God, knowing good and evil.'*
> (Genesis 3:5)

He still seeks to insinuate that God does not have our best interest at heart and hopes that he can cause us to doubt **God's integrity**.

The consequences of sin have been disastrous for mankind. Man's attitude towards God is no longer right and so man fears God and tries to hide from Him.

Adam Hid from God

> *'Then the man and his wife heard the sound of the LORD God as he was walking in the garden in the cool of the day, and they hid from the LORD God among the trees of the garden.'*
> (Genesis 3:8)

Sin is like a wall which keeps us apart and separated from God. He hates sin but loves the sinner. The only way to restore your relationship with God is to repent, which means to turn away from a sinful life and to begin to live the way God wants you to live.

Repentance starts at the cross, because if Jesus had not chosen to die for us then our sins would have taken us to hell. But Jesus chose to die for us on the cross in order that our sins might be washed away. This is the only way we can be saved.

> *'But if we walk in the light, as he is in the light, we have fellowship one with another, and the blood of Jesus Christ his Son cleanseth us from all sin. [8] If we say that we have no sin, we deceive ourselves, and the truth is not in us. [9] If we confess our sins, he is faithful and just to forgive us our sins, and to cleanse us from all unrighteousness.'*
> (1 John 1:7-9)

Appendix

If you recognise that you are a sinner and now wish to repent of your sins and become born again, which means to become a child of God and part of His family, then say the following prayer out loud:

> **Father, I recognise that I have sinned and lived my life without regard to Your word. But today I repent of my sin** (at this point mention specific sins that you need God to forgive you of). **I thank You that Jesus died on the cross for me. I thank You that He loves me this much. I now accept Him as my Saviour and my Lord. I thank You that the Bible says that if we confess our sins You are faithful and just and will forgive our sins and cleanse us from all unrighteousness. I thank You that I can have confidence that, now I have repented, You have forgiven me because You are a faithful God. I thank You that now I am born again.**

You are now a child of God, the best thing that could ever happen to anybody. If you are not already in a church please get in touch with a local Bible-believing church immediately. If you are not sure where to go then please write to me at 17 High Cross Street, St. Austell, Cornwall PL25 4AN or even better still phone me on (01726) 72282 and I will get back to you as soon as possible.